HEAR GOD'S THUNDER

MERIENNE LYNCH

Copyright © 2019 by Merienne Lynch.

Editorial Assistant
Pastor Joseph Anthony Schroeder

ISBN   Softcover   978-1-949723-92-2

All rights reserved. No part of this book may be reproduced or transmitted in any form or by any means, electronic or mechanical, including photocopying, recording, or by any information storage and retrieval system without express written permission from the author, except in the case of brief quotations embodied in critical reviews and certain other non-commercial uses permitted by copyright law.

Printed in the United States of America.

To order additional copies of this book, contact:
Bookwhip
1-855-339-3589
https://www.bookwhip.com

This book is dedicated to the
Three who wrote this book;
God The Father,
God the Son and
God the Holy Spirit.

CONTENTS

Introduction vii

Part I: The Church 1
Part II: Immigration 12
Part III: Understanding God: Do You Understand Me? 22
Part IV: Much To Be Said About The Heart 28
Part V: The Fear Of The Lord Is The Beginning Of Wisdom:
    It Is Reverence 38
Part VI: The Difference Between An Antichrist And
    The Man I Called 55
Part VII: Possess A Godly Attitude 64
Part VIII: Divided Against Yourself? 67
Part IX: Is Jesus Precious To You? 101
Part X: The Son Of Perdition 110
Part XI: Are You Positive He's Not Coming Yet? 124
Part XII: Some Call It Agape Love 134
Part XIII: Do You Touch Jesus? 145
Part XIV: Do You Know The Comforter? 149
Part XV 155
Part XVI 160
Part XVII 163
Part XVIII: A Portrait Of Love Between The Father, The Son
    Jesus Christ, The Holy Spirit And Our Beloved 165

About the Author 173
Thank you Message 175

INTRODUCTION

EACH AND EVERY one of you must examine your own hearts and see what you need. If you take the words of this book and apply them to everyone else but you, I promise you that this book will be no benefit to you. It is to lead you into all truth about yourself. Not about your neighbor.

From the beginning of this first part to the very end of the book these words are directly from the Lord as He spoke them to me, I wrote them; that is why there are quotation marks here at the beginning and at the end of the book. None of the words are mine; I am only the person that God used to write this book. If you want to get the most out of it, read it as though the Lord is speaking to you directly, the way you should read the Bible. Always keeping in mind how much the Lord loves you. So much that He is not willing to let you do anything to destroy your relationship with Him. All that is written is designed to lead you to examine yourselves and get yourself ready for the rapture.

Things need to be understood in the eyes of those who live in this time. This book is a Spoken Word from the LORD. You won't see through it quote and unquote's so much in the Bible but if you know your Bible you will recognize the words are His. From time to time, you will see that God the Father speaks or God the Son, or God the Holy Spirit this is why the book is dedicated to the Triune God. I know each One personally not that I am anything but that He chose it this way and actually I had no choice in the matter. He called me and dipped me into so many things that almost killed me and then healed and delivered me. Some of the descriptions of my relationship with Him when I would fight His will and His grace always overrode what I wanted or thought. It all started about 48 years ago. I am now 75 years old. When He came to me I did not know there was a God and no one ever told me about Him. And He came to me personally.

"Before I go on I want to say something here about the title and why she chose it. My word tells about dark clouds surrounding Me. I make it My habitation so that I AM not easily found by any man. My word also says that I AM a terrible God when I AM moved out of My place. If you're a parent you understand that if you are sitting and the children misbehave and you warn them and they refuse to listen what do you do? You get up out of your place and deal with them because that is the only thing that they will listen to. That fact proves that it is a fearful thing to fall into the hands of the Living God. I AM not dead. I AM alive! And many of My children need to realize that through this book. (end quote will be at end of the book).

PART I

THE CHURCH

Ephesians 1:22 And hath put all things under His feet, and gave Him to be the head over all things to the church.

23 Which is His body, the fullness of Him that filleth all in all?

THE WORD ALL means exactly that all. It doesn't mean just in any religion or church building or any particular place it means all. That is all over the world even when they don't gather have no one else with them the Lord Jesus is the head of every decision. Not the church body who decides the doctrine for itself. Not the preacher who formed it. Not the college that taught many things, not of the LORD. Not any Bible Study teacher. Not any Evangelist or any famous preacher because they wrote a book. It means every person is part of His body. And the fullness of Him fills all of them in all places; all times, all things.

My Son Jesus had twelve disciples. One of them He said upon this rock I will build My church. His church is His body not necessarily meaning a church building. The Rock He was speaking about was the confession that Jesus is the Christ the Son of the Living God. My Son. The Rock you build on is not Peter but on Christ Jesus and on knowing that He is the Son of the Living God.

If you read the Word of God you would see that God never spoke to the sinner harshly. He appealed to them and asked them kindly, and He spoke through Jesus with patience and love, but not so with His own, or those who were ungodly and claimed to be God's. To them, the Word says, "you generation of vipers, who hath warned you to flee from the wrath that is to come?" Concerning the baptism of repentance, the Lord said, Bring therefore fruits meet for repentance, and think not to say within yourselves that we have Abraham to our father for I say unto you that God is able of these stones to raise up children unto Abraham." My Son knew their hearts and how hardened they were and are even today in the church against the Truth which is Jesus Christ. He is the Truth, the Life, and the Way.

Even in the day where they walked and talked with Jesus those who claimed to believe, claimed to have God within them, they did exactly the same thing. They committed the very same error in thinking that they would escape His wrath by claiming to be saved by faith. And they committed those errors without any real hindrance from Me because it wasn't time yet to reveal the truth and set all of you free. I did warn you that the day would come when everyone would wonder who was really saved. No need to wonder. Every man is judged according to His knowledge of Me and what He did with it. Simple but you make it so complicated.

I am not against churches because every church is only as good as their leaders. I am not against any particular ministry or any such thing. I AM not calling out any individual preacher although many of them are doing the things that I will be speaking about.

I AM against false doctrines that preach and teach that if you don't follow their doctrine, or if you don't belong to their church that you can either be excommunicated or you are not saved. Since no church or doctrine died for you then no one has the right to tell you that if you do this or you do that; or if you don't do this or you don't do that; or if you don't go to church or if you do go somewhere else that you are going to hell because they did not die for you. Jesus did.

What I AM against is the deception of you claiming Me being with you when you know that your works are not done in truth. All I can say here clearly to you is that every man when they first go astray knows that they are going on the wrong path. They then harden their hearts until they know nothing anymore because every step after that becomes easier and easier until they are so deceived that they think they are right when they are wrong. As it says in Peter that judgment begins in the house of God and if the righteous scarcely be saved where shall the sinner and ungodly appear? And who do you think that I will visit first for sin? Well, I will tell you; the ones who claim the highest they are those who sit so high while my people suffer and endure oppression trying to please them desperately. And you know that time is short and soon the Anti Christ will appear. But there are things in this book about him that will benefit you to know exactly who to follow when that time comes. And it is so well upon its way but not yet time. Remember nothing will be revealed before it's time. No one knew about Judas until it was time to betray Jesus.

The first book that this vessel wrote was "Knowing the Terror of the LORD" (We Persuade all Men" 2 Corinthians 5:11) and it was written to prepare you for the rapture. You see you can't go with Him when He is ready unless you are ready and this is the time get ready. You know so many things are moving swiftly that you can hardly keep up with them. And when you are distracted with false lying media taking away from all My plans for this nation; you have distracted yourselves so that you can't hear or see or understand. Your answers are in Me and they are not written in how to prosper or how to have everything for yourself, nor are they in seeking to please Me by doing anything with other nations right now.

My people please Me when they believe that My Son died for them and trust Him to lead them to repentance, lead them into all truth about themselves first of all that they believe that He resurrected from the grave and His blood paid their price to get into heaven in His Name. Now that pleases Me because I can look at them and see the love they have for Him and remember what He went through to bring it all about. THEN I AM able to have great compassion for them.

You see immigration is no longer immigration. It has turned into the call of the Anti Christ to make this nation part of a one world government which he hopes to rule and reign over and you play right into his hands by hearing his call and not Mine. He has always been able to fool the church. Because he gets them tangled into things that have no value and no meaning such as traditions, rituals, and paying attention to the judgments of the eyes.

Through distractions of entertainment and social playing that you are intelligent; that you know and see what no one else does. It leads you into great error for your soul and endangers the lives of your loved ones. You listen to pied pipers who claim to be so wise and they are filled with envy, jealousy, hatred, deception. They who are adulterers call you President and adulterer and you love it to be so. If you didn't love it to be so you would have realized that he had those past sins whatever they may be which was none of your business under the blood of Jesus. And only an evil unbeliever would dare to pull them out. And only a foolish part of the church would be so foolish as to deny their own salvation through the blood by denying his. If you don't forgive him for his past I can't forgive you. And only the left who don't want Jesus or anything to do with God and guns would dare pull the stunt of using old tapes to trap him. But no marvel because the church that calls themselves by My name Christian are the ones that I will hold responsible. Not the media. I expect evil from them.

It was and is the church called Christian that I expected to be wise enough to see these things. But your own pastors can't see so how can you? All of you are too busy with the wrong things and in this book, I hope to correct that. To bring you all to a place that you see yourselves as you are so that I may lead you to repentance and not only save you but save this nation. You see if you repent then you become strong enough to destroy the works of Satan in this nation. But so far all of you are deceived.

It is no different a time than when I spoke to Jeremiah or any of My prophets who cried because you hardened your hearts to your own self-destruction. Read it; how the priests and the prophets lied to them and the people loved it just as most of you do now.

This book is being written in the hopes that you will wake up and see that I AM GOD and there is no other and I decided to answer the call of My true children of God who are true Patriots. A people who love My Son, love My Spirit and come before Me in TRUTH and no pretense and no lies. A people who not only were born here but respect their citizenship in a great nation that I nurtured for Myself. So I sent them a man who wants to drain the swamp and save My people and his name is President Donald Trump.

Yes, this nation was filled with many things that were wrong; but as you read you will see how I see My people who are called by My name who have humbled themselves and prayed and many turned from their wicked ways so that I could hear from heaven and heal their land. These people caused Me to marvel at their faith during an hour that no one should have had faith after all the atrocities done by those who hate this nation, hate this President, hate babies that are troublesome to the women who call themselves mothers. Hate, hate, and more hate. Causes them to dig into their bottomless pit of hell and pull out ways to destroy you, your President and this whole nation. If you doubt one tiny doubt then right now repent for this is all true.

"O My People, I want you to know that the responsibility of what took place in the church and why it is so important for you today to grasp what I Am about to say. I hold the leaders of the church completely responsible even though it has been handed down through many generations to bring forth people who are like the people that I will be speaking of; who walk and talk in error. Preaching and teaching the gospel the way they do has created more creatures using My Name without ever doing My will.

These people right now are spread all over the world still preaching and teaching how to live by faith without the first works of the heart to heal and deliver it and change it so they can be a people who reflect My Son's image. So that when Jesus comes back they will recognize Him for they will be like Him. Thus far they are only like those they have followed that led them into error following those in the media or Hollywood. Please pay attention to the scriptures given with this message right here so that I may open up your eyes that you may see that it is all too true that faith without works is dead. The first works are and were to be working out your own salvation with fear and trembling.

Not one person is able to help anyone else be led out of darkness into the light until they themselves are into the light. But sometimes like an assembly line you are led into a church where the pastors sit as kings and you become slaves to them and not to Me (the LORD). Their works were wicked in My sight and still are. Those sins were more serious than any sinner ever committed. I let the sinner go freely, knowing that when they heard about their sin they might take the opportunity to change.

Right now we are not talking about willful deliberate hypocrites but of a people who have been misinformed and lied to in order to keep them in line and keep their leaders rich. Believe this when I say this. Had the church not doing this that spirit never would have worked with the politicians. You live in a country where I the LORD meant it to be Christian and yet those who only claim God and do not have God are in control.

All the responsibility goes back to the leaders of the church who stand in judgment of a people that they taught in error. These creatures that make decisions that hurt My people put the church in such confusion that it also now has a nation filled with confusion; filled with envy and strife and every evil work. The Word said that those who follow such things as a sexual preference, not of Me are in a state of confusion.

I the Father had no intention of any of this happening when I gave so much to My church leaders through My Son. This book was written and designed to lead all leaders to repentance so that My people could be free to see, hear and understand the truth because only the truth will set them free. But you (you in speaking to church leaders) have them afraid to touch you and this ought not to be so. If after reading this book you can honestly say within your heart that you are doing My will in the churches then by all means continue. But if it touches your heart to see the truths then repent and I will be gracious and forgiving even though you have not been gracious and good to so many of My people. Remember what I said about hurting one of My Little ones who believe in Me.

Your prayer closets are filled with dead men's bones because you don't even know how to pray. You claim that you know that I Am a God of order and will never go outside My protocol. But you are outside it and out of order when you sit like a king and rob those who have less than you of the true gospel. I Am NOT for sale. I did not give you permission to sell my word by promising I will bless someone if they give you money.

I anointed you to understand and work with money but some of you are outrageously rich. This is why I told this "Prophet, Merienne Lynch" to make her first message to those "who call themselves My prophets". I want you to know that I Am doing a new thing. What seemed to work before will not work now. Because by buying and selling the gospel so many creatures that were not of God got a hold of it and used it against My people. This is what makes this book so crucial in teaching. There are those who listened to all the teachings that these so-called pastors and prophets made themselves rich with that it seems almost impossible to correct, but with the LORD all things are possible.

So there will be no mistakes or misunderstandings I will tell you what you did. I warned you through her not to continue and some of you said you would consider what she said and you knew it came from the LORD. I would not have warned you had I not known that if you would have prayed there would have been away for My people to get the information but not let it fall into the hands of those who used it to destroy this nation.

I can see no one understood why the left was so interested in how the right prayed in their emails. No one really understood that they took all that the great pastors taught and used it against this nation. They did things and if you look at it you will see. There was one of those who is guilty of the worst could confess that they were unstoppable. You taught that unstoppable message from the LORD, and so many more messages that belonged only to the disciples. You sold it to the masses which Jesus separated from. Jesus said in His word for you not to give that which is holy. And there just isn't anything holier than instructions on how to defeat Satan and it was used to defeat the right.

The LORD Jesus Christ spoke to the hypocrites and the ungodly and treated them very harshly by My Son; knowing very few of them would take the opportunity to repent. Jesus dealt with those who appeared to have God within but were empty and dead inside. Because He knew that they held on to believe that they were right when they were very wrong.

NONE of this at any time is written to expose any particular preacher or prophet or embarrass them or even hurt them. ALL of what is being written is to WAKEN them UP and turn them in the right direction; to help them to see the error of their ways. I AM treating them with more compassion than they ever treated the people that they use for their own gain. I did not make them a LORD over any man. No Lord over any woman in the household by her husband. Now, why would I make one a Lord to RULE OVER the church? Being a LORD or a leader are two different things. I warned you in Peter not to LORD over anyone.

When people sit so high in traditional teaching they sit high enough to judge when they should be using compassion. Knowledge puffs up. They use criticism when they should be reaching out for the truth to reach people. I watch in your services that claim I love how you do things agree with leaders who mock others who are less fortunate in understanding because he or she is so intelligent. You never realize what it is like to be less fortunate to not be able to figure things out. This is why I take nothing and make it into something so that all those who are above everyone are brought low. I took the vessel writing this book aside for years and taught her and she can't get in the presence of those who consider themselves great men of God because they would rob her of what I taught her and they would call her a protégé when she belongs to the Holy Spirit exclusively. I saw to it that no man could or would teach her so they could not claim she belonged to them. Many of you preachers that sold so many books people would bring them to her 20 at a time and tell her within the pages of all your books are the things that she taught them for years and she never read any of your books nor did she watch you on television or go to perhaps only one of your services.

You all live in a different day than ever before; a different time. There are many things on the earth alone; with so many things unleashed in so many ways. It is like the days of Noah when the evil saturated the earth so much that I had to take the creeping things into the Ark to start all over again. The evil affected them as badly as they do now. The fish, the plants, everything saturated with evil.

To live here takes the presence and power of Jesus Christ to overcome. Surviving won't do it. It is not enough. You in Christ that love My Son are more than conquerors even those preachers who have made great mistakes. Come let us reason together through this book and see if what I Am saying here is true? If you reach for Me with ALL your heart I will be there but after years of using nice words and nice songs to control or influence Me. After years of playing church and destroying My people and devastating their livelihoods promising things that you know that you can't possibly fulfill; you haven't made it easy. Many have spent their last penny giving and giving and giving because you instructed them to do so and now they have nothing and you have so much you waste in on your playthings. And you mock them even at the altar and call them stupid. And those who want to please Me think that I AM that evil that I would raise you to destroy the less fortunate with mockery. You get what you ask for when you think that I AM like you.

You need to grasp this whole situation and understand it no matter who you are. By realizing that Jesus Christ is the only One who can save you and seek Him with all your heart. Right here I am speaking from the pulpit to the pew. Man can't save you now. Not your pastor, not your teachers, not your mentors. Only One Who can save you now is Jesus Christ.

You will see farther on in this book how the political world and control ran parallel to the church's error. How and why I hold every church leader responsible and how they can be free. How you can be free. And it has nothing to do with the person who wrote this book. She is not asking you to follow her. She is not asking you for your money. She is not asking you to even buy this book. She understands that she is worthy of her hire; and that I Am the One who supplies her needs. She turned down millions so no one will say that any man-made Merienne Lynch rich. No man will control what she does with any money once it is donated and put in her hands to do as she chooses. The churches were controlled by those who gave money into it and were heard to the point that the pastors were afraid to preach and teach the true gospel or they would lose their donations and congregations. And in making this unfortunate decision they will lose them anyway. They will lose their flow of being able to deceive enough that many will be paupers. I have instructed this vessel that if I lay it upon any heart to give to her to continue this ministry then, by all means, take it. Because there are many things I do want her to do. But if you are not led by Me then don't give a penny because there is no promise of a greater blessing than you can receive in the word yourself by obeying My Word.

THIS PART WAS TAKEN OUT OF FIRST BOOK:

The first book was written so that you may see how I see, how I feel, think, act, and hear through all the things that you go through; by using her as an example of a relationship with My Son. It was designed to enlighten you to the truth that these things are real and no man can tell you that you are going to die; you are going to hell, because no man died for you. No man can say one thing about your life, because prophecy is not for personal use. A true prophet is only confirmed to what you personally have had coming from Me. No prophet gives you anything. They don't give you blessings; (I THE LORD) is the only One Who has that power. Oh, they lay hands on you and say they do but remember they give you who and what they are and you will become like them because you chose to believe them and not My word.

First of all, don't at any time think I AM ever referring to any particular person that I do not name here. You think you know who I AM talking about that is your business, but I did not say it to you. I might mention past with what some people did, but still, I did not mention their names because I AM against no man, no woman; I AM against sin.

You are about to read how I visited this vessel and she endured My glory and My terror. The way every man who claims My name will in eternity. The way Paul the apostle endured it when he was on the road to Damascus. No matter what anyone thinks, how anyone prays, no matter how they believe nothing can ever come back on her for what she is writing because Satan has the power to do many things, but the one thing that he can't do is imitate My glory and My terrifying Presence. He can make you feel fear in the flesh. But as you feel fear in the flesh you have a witness in your Spirit that it isn't Me. No matter how it tries to consume you, you know that it isn't Me. But when I come on the scene there is no doubt that it is I the Lord. You will never be able to say it wasn't Me. Remember this for this is important to you.

There comes a time in every life that I VISIT. You won't know what day or what hour but you will know that I came upon you. Because I love you and don't want you to perish I will do with you what I did with her over and over again. You see it took many times not just one time. To burn out the sin; to destroy all that was in her heart, mind, spirit, and body I had to visit many times and when I touched her everything that was not of Me was taken off of her. Had she been shallow and played she would have had nothing. She would have been left with nothing except the power to come to Me and repent and change her ways. She welcomed the experience and after the first time, she knew that I loved her so much just as I do you that I did not want her to perish in any deception, any wrong of any kind.

When I got done with her what remained was Me. My Spirit, and My word within her. It didn't take months, weeks it took years to perfect it over and over and over. So if you want to imitate go ahead because I promise you that you won't like it or want it. She loved it because she knew. But will I show you if your heart seeks only to bring things to yourself to make yourself like her when I want you to be you? The pretending spirits that run rampant in the church. Those spirits that plagiarize another person's walk and use it for self-gain and like a vampire that sucks the blood out of a person who labored long and hard to get close to Me you walk away leaving them in the dust as though I AM with you forgetting that I AM

GOD. And when you steal what you think is another person's anything then you, in the end, have the loss, not Mine. I keep her; will I keep you?

Those of you that think you are doing My will never be looking at or teaching the negative part of repentance and turning away from your wicked ways. Calling and teaching conviction as though it is of the devil when the conviction is a work of the Holy Spirit. Those of you who hold the hands of others who worship another god and you teach them aspects and principles of Me. You also swear that you will always help them. I promise you they learn it for your destruction and believe Me what you are doing is not compassion. It is misguided and it is disobedience. That is not what I called any of you to do. I called you to be kind, use wisdom and teach godly fear enough to bring souls to Christ. If you have nothing more than a positive message and you lead others to that and they follow you remember this that I AM GOD and you can't take My place and teach and preach against Me.

PART II

IMMIGRATION

But if any provide not for his own, and especially for those of his own house, he hath denied the faith and is worse than an infidel (I Timothy 5:8)

WHAT I AM about to say will seem to some heartless but I assure you it is the truth. There are a people who are very much like the people who walked on the earth at the time My people the Jewish "peculiar" people were being called to Me. They are on the earth today in the same condition, worshipping another god who is no god; another god in the sense of any god who is not Me. For I AM the LORD thy God and there was never any before Me or besides Me. I AM GOD. Because I Am God I chose a people who would love and worship Me the way I chose. I put my laws inside of their hearts the way I wrote them on the tables of every true believing Christian. I chose the Jew and I chose the Christian.

Jesus told you that you did not call Him; He called you. If you love Jesus then I (God the Father) revealed to you Who Jesus is and that He is the Son of the Living God. Jesus said that flesh and blood did not reveal it to Peter that Jesus was and is the Christ. Living inside of you is so important. There is such a difference between death and life in the human flesh of every person. Living and breathing in the Word are JESUS CHRIST. He is the Word and He lives and breathes in you if you let Him in. And the word became flesh and dwelt among us. Just as the word becomes flesh and dwells in you if you let Him. Not just some of Him but ALL of Him. He is not about what you wear, what you put on, how you look or even what you eat, what you give or don't give, go to church etc..

I changed all that In the epistles, where Peter was told to kill animals that he called uncleanly. He was told to kill and eat. Some people to this day don't eat certain meats don't realize what I said in that instance.

I changed so much in the gospels when Jesus said: "But I say unto you". But you follow it as a dead God once was; not as a "Living God" right now. Jesus said, "you have heard it has been said". Then He said, "but I say unto you…" The Antichrist doesn't believe that Jesus lives in the flesh through His children. Consider this when you force yourself to read your Bible. When you force yourself to obey rather than work with Me to work it all out of you through confession, forgiveness, and repentance; when you force yourself to repeat the word over and over striving to put something in you that only I AM able by grace to do within you. Then you deny Me the power to help you die to what you think, belief, understand, used to do etc. And let Jesus live instead of you. And some of you that behave so badly I wouldn't believe My Son is inside of you. For Jesus to come you have to die to self there is no room for you and Him. It is as simple as that. What He would do and what you would do are two different things. For so many of you, it is easier to name it and claim it. Death to the flesh is very painful. Doing what the LORD wants is the same as He did for you when He said "Father, not My Will, but Thy will be done."

Why did I say seem to be heartless? Because the Word which is Jesus has the same laws that the Ten Commandments had such as thou shalt not kill, thou shalt not bear false witness. So important to know this country was based completely on those laws which are the Laws of God. The words in those commandments breathe life into every individual's souls. Their souls come alive with knowing it is wrong to lie, steal covet, murder etc. Without those truths the person who claims any other god is soulless. There are no boundaries, no truths for Jesus is the Way the Truth and the Life. They actually have no way of discerning the truth from a lie. No way of discerning what is good or bad without the guidelines from the Bible. A Word that has been in existence for thousands of years because it keeps anyone who believes in it filled with all that is good, all that is righteous, all that is true. Are you to go around telling everyone or treating everyone less than yourself because you know these truths and you think they don't? NO, that is where I said don't brag or puff yourself up because I AM able to cut you off the way I did those who refused to believe.

I sat and ate with sinners, and homosexuals were at that table and they were not won by Me pointing out their sin. My Son did not go into detail the way some preachers have from behind the pulpit and described every evil act. Especially since I said in the word that it is a shame to speak of those things done in the darkness; they were won by the righteousness in Jesus just being there. Believe me, they were won not lost because even if they didn't understand it or see it clearly when faced with My Son Jesus Christ they did later when I The Holy Spirit spoke to them to convince them of their sins so that they could go to My Son Jesus. I have been in the presence of prayer meetings where the pastors describe such evil when it would have been better for them to go into detail to describe the things in the gospels. You know why they don't because they don't know Me. If they did they would never speak any evil from behind any pulpit.

This country obeyed the law and fulfilled the law by those I sent to keep them in order. Many of you who speak in church about order don't understand the order. I sent them that are in the law to help you to obey the law with simple basic truths that protect all mankind. Without those laws, you will and they do make murder a matter of opinion. Many of them in the womb had a mother rub their belly and chant kill Americans, and kill Jews. When they come out they have a strong sense of soullessness. They would kill you without batting an eye and you would be foolish to try to witness to them for there is nothing there to witness to. We are not talking about someone who has any sense within their soul about right or wrong. It isn't there. In the day years ago people grew up with some sense even the worst criminals. Now it is not so.

The enemy of your soul is so subtle and so wise compared to you and your basic teachings in the church about things that don't matter to Me. Like I said if you wear a skirt or pants or a man wears this or that or if you come off the street and have nothing you are not accepted because of how you dress. Or if you wear makeup and think Jezebel was a devil because she wore makeup you have no sense of what is right or wrong. I said to judge righteous judgment and not according to the eyes. All that has to be taught to women is modesty make sure you don't show your nakedness. If an arm or a part of a leg disturbs you then get on your knees and pray and see what is wrong with you. You pay attention to all the wrong things and destroy the innocent and let the guilty go free. That is one of the conditions of your nation. And it all started in the church.

Church leaders should have protected the innocent and condemned the guilty but as we go on you will see how this nation became this way when I intended it to be Christian. This is why the enemy is fighting so hard against these two nations because I chose them and the lawless and disobedient want their own god, their own laws which are no laws. And there are those who labored to make this a lawless country. They knew exactly what they were doing. They knew if they kicked Me out of their organizations; or if they destroyed history; and if they could convince the young who have no idea of what is going on, if they can control the money, if they can dictate lies through the media like they always have THEN the enemy of your soul would have this country with the rest of them. You would not be able to see any difference between them.

This is why the struggle between the families a man of God or woman of God already married then saved wind up with the ungodly one who rejects Christ striving to pull them down. Because if they succeed in proving you are not Christian they then feel justified in their evil deeds. It is very much like the alcoholic who comes home and fights with the spouse until the spouse can't take it anymore then the alcoholic feels peace and say within themselves. "See they deserve it they are just like me and only pretending to believe in Christ." By engaging in a fight with anyone like this you are ripping your own testimony to shreds and they are helping you and you blame them when you made a wrong choice.

This country wasn't so much built upon immigration and the ability to come here and fulfill the American dream. For many who did so much evil came here then. This nation became great because the laws were formed by the laws of God in the Bible that you put your hand on to swear to tell the truth etc. This land became great because the Christians in this country knew that I loved Israel and that I would bless this nation if they blessed the Jews.

When My people in this country who did not want to obey My will in My word My way for Jesus is the Way they then turned to the media to tell them who to vote for. The ignorant and disobedient listened intently as though these people were so intelligent and you will see them even now claim on some of these most abominable liars on television telling you that they are the only adults; you let them dictate to you who to vote in office and because it was allowed loved and enjoyed, and no one really bothered to seek Me for it. Pride reigns; they say we are the only ones who know and see the truth because we are educated and because we are intelligent and this is evil in their doings. The disobedient don't want to work so they made up these lies rather than seek Me. In their minds, they could pretend with an agreement with evil media that they are more intelligent.

Read the word what I think of man's wisdom who doesn't want Mine because they don't need Me. They could pretend to be Christians because they went to church or worked in the church and deceived themselves because they did so they thought that they were pleasing to Me. Believing My word as it is would have done a better job. NONE of what they did or does please Me. They might as well have stayed home. You sing, dance, shout and go and choose evil knowing they are killing babies, knowing they are doing evil and you even give your money to them while My people have nothing. You pretend in the church among yourselves and pat yourselves on the back on how great your worship of Me is and then vote for someone who murders babies. Where is your common sense? Oh, because evil media can bring up things of a man's past and hide their own evil you decide which is the weightier matter? Who bewitched you? The media! Causing you not to see or obey the truth. They are still adulterers and adulteresses calling out your President. Like a child pointing so constantly in the hopes you never see or know what they have done and are doing in secret. But the day will come that they will know that I AM GOD and I do know what they do.

Immigration now is a matter of people wanting what you have worked for all your life. You worked for it. I blessed many of you with it and now they want it. And the only person who stands between what is happening is Jesus in the man I called. By the time he got into office, the media controlled many ignorant people and still do. They were so afraid that the people would see and know that he actually by nature even if he had not gotten saved knew how to behave himself and knew what was true and understood what was going on. And many of you forgot I came to lead the sick to repentance.

If the man knows abortion is a murder that alone should have been enough to show you the difference between him and a murderer. By the time he got in office the laws were being undone so that the lawless could do exactly as they chose and they knew all they had to do was kick Me out. God and guns they kicked hard at. My greatest warriors in defense of this nation such as the Marines have a belief that they fight for the right, fight for freedom, fight for the honor. They are in existence because they believe in God and country.

Every Patriotic heart and also every Christian recognizes how he thinks and feels. This is why he can't be imitated. The enemy of your soul cannot pretend to be what he actually is. Nor can he pretend to be what My people are. So they look at the surface of things and try to lie about it and when they could not find the answer they decided to "character assassinate him". And many of you helped them by sitting in front of the media and listening to their contrived lies. They had and still don't and still won't for I will not give any of it to them unless they repent.

No one can see unless I open their eyes and I am not about to open the eyes of someone who is out to destroy My children. Just by being him and by My people being them there is that connection. Unfortunately, some of My people began to destroy what I revealed to them giving into the lies against the truth in every patriotic Christian. Getting ready to meet My Son in the air; there are more of them than ever before and that will continue to grow. Even if they shut off all form of communication, burn the Bible no one can shut God the Father, God the Son, God the Holy Spirit down. No one can imitate it, buy it, or steal it. ALL they can do is pretend they have it and some of My more ignorant children are deceived by them.

When you let hoards of people who care nothing for their own children or country and the lawless make it look like they go through great sacrifice by leaving their children behind or sending them ahead or using them to get a birthright here. Many of those children are being raped and abused. Don't tell Me they love or care for anyone but themselves. When you can use your child and sacrifice it to get more in greed you are not seeking a better place you are seeking to take a land that is not yours. But these liars who have controlled for so long don't want you to find that out. So they play their games in lies and it is up to you to recognize the truth from a lie. How are you going to do that? You apparently left off common sense because it should have told you the truth about this great flood of people who don't care for their own won't care for yours. They will do so much worse with yours.

In this book is a lot of reality of scripture written in a language that anyone can understand today. When My people who are called by My name will humble themselves and turn from their wicked ways, I will hear from heaven and heal their land. This nation is your land and it is in terrible need to be healed. Listen up right here. Heal their land which is this country that they were born in. Not some country that they go to in order to heal and deliver people who are not their people. Not that I Am against that but take care of your own first. That is why I have made it America first. Listen why I the LORD made it America First. I led your President to make America first so that My people could fulfill My desires for this country and her children. Then do for others. What good are you if you are completely destroyed by those who have no understanding except being wanton? You say they need. I say they want. They would have been blessed to be born here had I called them here. Don't you see?

What gospel are you preaching to other nations when you lead them in globalism? What gospel are you preaching when you teach them that God is with them to invade and take something that doesn't belong to them? Is it called "coveting other people's goods gospel?" because you covet other people's money by selling My gospel you can only give others what you have therefore you fed them this. Wake up! You preach and teach what you are! And many in those nations heard you tell them that I gave them permission to take because you taught them how to take, and lied that I AM with them. What you do you preach and teach. And without ever thinking about the people you preach to or what would happen to this nation you continue for years thinking that you can desert this country and take in others until you have no country anymore. Listen to Me the person who picked up orphans because they have no food. And takes from their own children mouths until there is nothing left for none of them what in the world have they accomplished? I would have delivered them, in the end, had I been with them to desert their children but they turned their backs on the truth in Me. If that person who isn't looking to be seen, to show they are of God to everyone by the sacrifice of her own children then why didn't they pray that someone who had the means would have taken those orphans in? I promise you I had it planned to send someone who could do the job but no you want to be something in someone else's eyes. Why? Because you are taught that you don't love God if you don't desert your own. I did not teach that I said if you don't take care of your own first that you were worse than an infidel. Where is your common sense? Don't you see the socialism that forms out of the church???

I am not speaking that it was wrong to go into poor countries to help people. I am saying it was wrong to go into those countries and promise them things that you should have been used to heal here. I the LORD declares this day I never call anyone into other countries until you personally feed your poor here. Until you deliver the gospel to My people here. It is a betrayal to Me and this country to go into other countries while you have such hell going on with the children of this country whom you have neglected. There are poor here that you should have taken care of first. Right now the youth of this country is listening to men who have been known to say that every woman in America dreams of being raped by these terrible people. Doesn't that tell you how sick this man really is??? The young can't see it because of the lack of History being taught blinds their eyes. Who in the end will pay for all of this?

A few years back some of you had the gall to go into Mexico and preach that I was going to deliver them and split the USA in half and give everything to Mexico. This country has enough poor in it that it can't take on another country until it first deals with their own. This is where your invasive caravans were born. Preaching without responsibility for what you used the gospel for. Thinking I was with you when in reality you were all by yourself. This is where they can come here and think to take over. Who did this terrible thing to lie to them that I would desert My own in this country? You are the reason they have the gall to scream and yell that I Am with them when I Am NOT. They have the gall to yell that only God can stop them as though I am with them to invade this country and take over My people here and make it their very own. Have I not told you that I would judge the world and that you were to take care of your own?

Didn't I tell you in the Word that the poor you will ALWAYS have with you but you will not ALWAYS have Jesus Christ? While this was and is a Christian nation all leaders of the church were called here. This is why they want more jets because they have no sense of what is important and this is why they can ask for more money for it because My people have no sense of what is true and not true. These invaders from Mexico have no respect or love for their own families or country because they were taught that God is with them if they desert their children or send some by themselves. To be raped and destroyed. Where did this sickness come from??? This was born out the lack of understanding of Me. Not knowing what I want, what I think or feel about such things. And how does that happen? I called her to give the first message to the prophets who even now they are not accurate. They speak from their fleshy hearts and limited knowledge of Me.

Where do you think that these hoards of people in this nation who once attended church, who once listened to preachers which I call creatures to tell them if they came into some money don't pay their bills? Use the money to enjoy. Because there was to be a transference of money to take from those who earned it and give it to a generation of people who thought because of the past they were entitled. So what did these people do? They got tired of waiting on God to do it because I the LORD do not steal from one to give to another. So they decided to covet to the point that they dared say that we are coming to take from you what you have. This didn't just happen overnight.

It happened in secret with the church leaders of the race deciding that I was evil enough to take from those who earned it to give to those who really don't want to work. This country has one thing called capitalism and if you work long enough and hard enough you can and will fulfill the American dream. But there are those who refuse to work and want the easy way out so they make up lies fed by the media and their church leaders that God feels sorry for them and I will as the LORD supply what doesn't belong to them. What in the world ever happened to "Thou shalt not covet thy neighbors goods". Can't you see how far that many of you have taken the gospel and destroyed the truth in it? Why did that happen?

In the voting booth. You voted for gender in the past, you voted for the race, you voted for every evil reason but none did their homework to find out if how serious I take murdering and mutilating babies. How serious I as God take worshipping another god in the White House. To you and to them you might as well have thumbed your nose at Me and said: "GOD IS DEAD". He doesn't see, he doesn't hear, He doesn't know, nor does He understand.

Well, I AM here today to tell you and all those who think that they can or will invade this nation and continue to take what is not theirs that I AM GOD and I see, I hear, I know, I understand and I will repay saith the LORD. REPENT before it is too late. Dump everything and anything that is connected to murdering babies. Drop everything and anything that is connected to the things that are against the Living God. And don't you dare say that I told you to hate the homosexual and that they deserve to die. Because if anyone deserves to die it is the one who claims the highest and lives the lowest.

As church bodies, it is evil to stand at funerals and hold signs saying "God hates you". How DARE you. What do you know about what I hate? I hate your sin of hate. Hating the sin and hating people are two different things. I don't ever hate any person. My Son died to give them an opportunity to go into heaven so how can I hate. I hate what they do, where they go sometimes what they say. But some of those people you hate and dare say need to be killed were sexually abused from the day they were born. And what are you going to do with the tortured children with evil parents to make them transgender? You going to kill them also and think you are doing My will? I grant you the fact that many blatantly, openly choose to be who and what they are. But I assure you many were brought into this world with curses on their lives so bad that the influence took over from past generations or evil parents. I said it is Luke that you don't know what kind of person that I AM. They thought I should call fire down from heaven to deal with disobedience to their will. Your worse you think I kill people because you judged them to go to hell. Judge not lest ye be judged you will get the same measure I promise you.

PART III

UNDERSTANDING GOD: DO YOU UNDERSTAND ME?

> The fear of the LORD is the beginning of wisdom: a good understanding has all they that do His commandments: His praise endureth for ever. (Psalm 111:10)

NONE OF THIS is written to destroy anyone or their ministry. It is written to lead those who can see through the mirror of this Spoken Word that has the power to convict them and lead them to repentance. No one no matter how high or how low it is not My desire to hurt them in any way. Therefore if you use this to do that it is upon you for you will answer to Me because you see I AM GOD. And I chose to come this way because no one would or could listen. You all loved your ears tickled by those who lied to you and stole from you. If I were to appear before you right now; no matter how brave you think you are. No matter how close you think you are to Me. No matter how many years or how many years you studied or faithfully went to church. If I appeared before you the way I did this prophet you would fall to your knees and be terrified because I AM GOD and so powerful that no one can stand before Me. You wouldn't just fall over backward. You could not imagine what it is like. The way Moses felt, the way this prophet felt; the way many others felt. Your so far away from Me that you may never feel it until it is too late to repent today. Seek Me today to change your ways and stay there until the job is done.

I AM also saying very plainly many of you knew this prophet. You read her book and you refused to allow her to reach the church. You refused to help her to be used of Me to open the hearts and minds of My people. My people saw this book and refused to read it because they didn't like my word on the title. The fear of the LORD is giving Me the reverence I so deserve. Yet all of you chose to listen to your teachings even in your colleges that if it doesn't comfort then it is not of the LORD because the Holy Spirit is a Comforter. How ignorant can you be?? How can you say that when if you read you would have seen that the job of My Holy Spirit is to convince you of your sins read it in Jude. That is called conviction.

Whatever appeases the flesh is the path you take when I told you repeatedly in My word which you claim to read every day in your devotional. It is a devotional that many of you use like those who read their horoscope and look for guidance from the enemy of your souls. You do the same exact thing with My word because you don't really want Me; you want what you want and when you answer for it you will get what you don't want because you will have to die to the flesh anyway in order to go into heaven with My Son.

The first book that I called her to way back in 2002; I told her plainly that My church is in trouble. They know how to pray for a new car or home but they do not know Me and when I come to convict them of their sin that they may repent and be saved. They chose to listen to their church leaders lie to them so they say "Get away from me you devil!" My Word taught for you to be led to repentance and turn from your wicked ways. And when you suffered you blamed everyone but your own sinning. You did exactly what your leaders did for they sinned in secret and blamed everyone but themselves, therefore, they shut the door to repentance and could not change even though they pretended they did not want to change their hearts or their minds.

And what did I ask these hypocrites to do? 'Bring fruit meat for repentance.' Fruit is something that begins as a seed and grows. Fruits are something that you have to cultivate, and water, and expose to just enough sun. Now if you were able to only name it and claim it. Only able by some miracle to obtain the fruits of the Holy Spirit, there would be no reason to call them fruits. The ungodly are those who claim to have Me in their heart but they have fruits that are obviously wicked. These people became so wrapped up in believing that they could toy with Me, pretend before Me and man, to have something that they do not have, they deceived themselves, deceived each other, but never Me. The greatest revival isn't how many healings or miracles are seen. My people can get that within themselves through My Spirit. Those are for the unsaved to believe, who have never heard of the conversion of the soul to Jesus.

I Am speaking of the of the revival that changes the heart within you towards Me, and revives the soul with their relationship with My Son and gets cleansed through the blood of Jesus Christ, and allows Me to continue the operation by permitting Me to create within My church a new heart, one that is faithful and upright in spirit; a spirit that will never turn away from Me. A true conversion comes from the Holy Spirit conviction and going into the Word to work out your salvation with fear and trembling. Were you taught to do that or were you taught to play with the Holy Spirit as though it was a game and go into a room and have three or four people tell you their visions because they were all prophets. So you sit there and listen and guess what My Spirit was there to send strong delusion to the ones so called prophesying and the ones receiving because they received not the love of the truth. It is exactly as My Word says "strong delusion" so that you would receive and believe a lie. You people have used prophecy as a tool to play with the way you used psychics and séances.

Don't any of you realize that prophecy is not written in stone because man has a free moral agency to change his mind or heart at any time he so wishes? Don't you see that the prophecy that you go from church to church to have a word spoken over you is a word that only you can fulfill? Do you understand that because it sounds good and it sounds like I promised you that; if you don't answer the call and become obedient it is nothing more than just words spoken that go empty into the air and never come true because you never obey Me? Do you not know that if you see any tragedy, any horrible happening, any atrocity etc. that your first duty as a prophet is to bring it to Me and pray with all of your heart that if there is any way for it not to happen ask Me for intervention? Or do you just take off and run with it to prove that you are a prophet with a word from the LORD? Are you one of those who doesn't see that intervention is My desire rather than to destroy? Do you know Me at all??? If you did; you would not be so quick as to run to tell it but you would be very quick to pray that destruction will not come if possible.

I am amazed at the amount of preacher, prophets, teachers, evangelists, and so-called apostles give prophetic utterances against others who they judge and condemn for not obeying when they themselves are guilty of disobedience. You know I marvel at faith but I also marvel at the ability of some of you to pretend to yourselves that you are something that you are not an act as I will never come to correct you. I have to correct you; you leave Me no choice if I want you to get into heaven then I must correct you.

Did you know that when you run to tell it that you are feeding power to it to come to pass? That if you would have tarried quietly; holily between you and me that perhaps all could have been avoided. There is much to be understood on how not to feed the wrong things and I won't teach it here. Those kinds of things were used by the left from all the teachings concerning the Bible and that is exactly how they defeated the Republicans on the right. I AM not talking about Rhino spies.

This part is about the fear of the LORD and I will tell you here and now. Those of you that saw clearly and plainly in the beginning that I sent Trump to deliver this nation and you decided to listen to the media character assassinate him because they could not tear him down nor could they say what he was doing to rid the country of the swamp creatures was wrong so they played with your evil minds telling you things that if someone said those things about your past and many of you did worse than he did you would not have expected him, who knew nothing as you knew about God to act immediately like a saint.

Some of you weren't born when they had a big scandal on what they were doing with the pages in Washington. For people to act like they don't sin is unbelievable. When you point out that he sinned remember so did you before you found My Son. With the whole world against him, those of you who call yourselves by My name decided to come against him and control him when he had more than you did all of your so-called Christian life. Look back through those tapes that I the LORD made sure were taken that he knew and understood years before this exactly what was going on. Media doesn't show that they only want you to pay attention to certain things because they know your pride before all men as you confess that you are a Christian you don't want anyone to know your past. I promise you if you continue to listen to them about his past you will have yours exposed to all. You should never have listened to the evil and fed it. You helped them destroy him and you will reap what you sowed if you don't repent now.

He was and is the only one who desires to help the Christian. Oh, I don't want to go on for what you have done to this man is that evil in My sight. I sent you a man who could have and would have saved this nation. And you did to him what the hypocrites did to My Son. And it is only My grace and mercy that keeps him and you will see him high and lifted up while you yourself will face judgment unless you repent today for today is the day of salvation.

How do you think that it looks to me when for how many years you just let a godless individual handle everything because some of your wouldn't vote then when you did even at this midterm election you gave power to those who clearly go against the things that are important to Me. Perhaps not to you but in My word it is clear that it is important to me. When anyone can hold any book and call it holy and you know the teachings in that book are far from holy. My book doesn't say kill the infidel; Mine doesn't tell you those things. When My Son walked on the earth He did say protect yourself so you need a gun just like He told His disciples to sell all they had and buy a sword. If someone invades your home you have a God-given right to protect yourself. The only place you are to turn the other cheek was among the brethren. Where is common sense? Why would I deliberately want My people slaughtered by those who are evil?

You should have seen it from the beginning and have had no one tell you. You should have recognized Me working with him. But after years of voting and keeping evil in place, you decided that this evil media who influenced you and destroyed this nation all these years must be right. SICK, SICK, SICK is the kind of nation that permits and helps destroy the only one that I sent. Haven't you seen the hatred and violence that the media has incited by feeding hatred and lies every day?

A leader from within slowly destroys this nation and none of you spoke up. None of you ever lifted one finger to say "Hey, this is wrong! This is our country and the laws you are changing are the ones that keep it doing what is right." But no, you felt America must pay the way he did and his Pastor did and you forgot you're an American and the only one who could have changed things through prayer by faith. That was too much like work; after all, you had your entertainment and sports shows and poor you worked so hard that you deserved to ignore this nation until it was too late. You have your evil Hollywood stars that are working so hard to continue to destroy this nation by changing the laws. Talented liars and pretenders meant more to you that My Son. Who is going to suffer because of all of this?

PART IV

MUCH TO BE SAID ABOUT THE HEART

> The heart is deceitful above all things, and desperately wicked: who can know it?
> (Jeremiah 17:9)

HAVEN'T YOU NOTICED that the wicked never run out of ways to destroy, hate etc.? This is why it is called a bottomless pit which the enemy dwells. Evil never runs out of evil. Once it is touched it waxes worse and worse and until they repent of the first lie if they can ever find it or want to find it they can't change and don't want to change. There is a difference between willingly ignorant, and truly ignorant are those who don't know and it has never been revealed to them yet, and those who willfully and deliberately turned their back on Jesus Christ and worse yet began to speak evil of My Holy Spirit. They are soulless not just because they have no written law of My word in them but because what they had destroyed it deliberately so they could have what they lusted for. Some in this condition are too afraid to blaspheme my Spirit they have not truly turned their backs on Me. But others who hate Me have no desire to repent it is all too late.

    THE HEART is where the grapes of wrath are stored. The heart is above all exceeding wicked without God. The proof is looking around at those who have no soul. When I say no soul they have no sense of right or wrong. They make up their own rules their own beliefs and call it right. This is why Jesus is called the King of Righteousness for in His word is the only truth about how to live righteously. ALL else is another god, ALL else is another gospel which isn't another gospel and many of you speak and preach another gospel through the traditions, rituals, and doctrines that I will prove in that great day are not of ME. Don't mistake what I AM saying here. There are those who from the very beginning of their walk with the LORD never saw, understood or received the truth. Too many things taught about positive thinking, prosperity and too many people rejected from the church for not following the traditions and rituals man has built.

I spoke plainly to this vessel that it wasn't I the LORD who made a difference between a prophet and what you call a prophetess. From the very beginning, you paid no attention where I taught in My word that when it comes to the gifts of God flowing through a vessel it doesn't matter if it is a man or a woman. I see only a willing vessel. Since the day My Son walked on the earth, you will see proof of the attitude towards women with the woman at the well-spoken about in the gospel. Jesus knew the heart of man and never committed to them. I willfully and deliberately chose a woman to prove to these men who believe that I gave them the power to destroy women if they dared to believe that I would call them to a task such as this. I said in this book that I only call a woman when a man won't go. No one wanted to go where this vessel was willing to go.

They pretend they have respect for women who are quiet or soft-spoken or whatever. But you see I do exactly as I choose. And although you may think you are a king. I AM GOD and will remain so. Some things in the Bible are to be examples but they are for the ones I call to those places to be those things. He told you about eunuchs let he who could receive it receive it.

PLEASE read Jeremiah. You will see how I spoke to My prophet. You will see how I dealt with the sins of My people being deceived by their leaders and love to have it so. Don't you see it even now? How they worship actors, gladiators such as football and basketball? Don't you see how they are willing to pay anything for their entertainment while the people they worship are rich and they are poor? Don't you see in most of your movies how all dark and evil everything is and yet you still pay money to be entertained? And while you are entertained; this country was going down deeper and deeper until one man was willing to face the whole world to change it? Let that sink down deep into your being. He chose to stand against the evil he knew was going on in this world. Not just in this nation.

He has a family that he loves and grandchildren. He knew that if someone did not do something they would go down the drain with the oppression and atrocities of the swamp creatures and he knew there was no other nation who could or would keep their sovereignty that his children could enjoy the life that he had. The choices that he knows existed for every man came with the price of obeying the laws. And those laws as I told you in My word were made for the lawless. But the lawless chose to destroy those laws and you who voted him and others who hate Me into the office for any reason helped them do just that. And all of you will stand before Me in that great day and answer for what you did in that voting booth and the consequences not only on other people but your children for generations to come. All these years this nation grew more and more corrupt and all these years you as a Christian let the media tell you what was what; who is who; as though they are so much more knowledgeable than you. As though they would tell you the truth but they didn't and they don't know. They hate the truth the way they do now and they are like the left they are terrified of losing all their power so they hang on for dear life and don't care if you die at the hands of criminals; just so long as they get their money and power.

And many of you are so ignorant that you actually believe these people care about telling the truth when you see them lie and trash this President unmercifully. Read Psalm 18 with the merciful I will show Myself merciful. With the forward, I will show Myself forward. Froward means willful so when you get willful with God I will get willful with you. When you have no mercy and listen to what you know are blatant lies just so that you can have your way with your sexual preference, or with that baby who is nothing but trouble to you. Those people are bad enough, but I AM talking about the so-called Christian who could have done something about it. Revelation 13 is real. You are bringing so much on your head and you and your children will have to lose your heads in order to stay alive. And these kinds of people who will demand that you deny Christ; which you right now have already denied in your votes. They will kill you anyway. They are vile but they hate homosexuals. They are vile enough to destroy babies; little girls and yet they are holy??? You let them in your schools to teach a religion that goes against Me. And you expect

Me to bless you. When I say let them you do it by voting people who fight for them and support them.

How foolish you are that you voted for criminals and evil lying people for years and years and years and when this one came along many of you in your prayer meetings even with the women prayer meetings claimed you wanted to vet him. WOW. His beliefs were not enough. They were righteous even before he knew Me and yet they were not enough. Did you ever have another leader willing to stand against killing babies?

You people who refused to vote saying that you had no one to choose from because both were evil because you believed the character assignation of the President because they knew he was doing right for the country and they knew they were losing their power over and they knew there was no other way except to feed this unreasonable hatred. Many of you ate it and if you didn't, you saw I called him and then you began to doubt. You paid more attention to what the enemy of your soul fed you than what I revealed to you. Believing for years that you had nothing to choose from causing you to do exactly what I wrote about in Malachi 3. How, when you throw your hands up in the air and say what is the use of following God; then what you are doing is you then allow the wicked to do exactly what they choose. You should have got on your knees and prayed to ask Me to give you wisdom. I promised to give you wisdom all you had to do was spend some time with Me.

But your leaders lie and say they believe but when the time came for them to believe they said they were to keep it separate and not mix into the politics of the nation. To a point that is correct like I said I did not call a preacher to the White House to lead this nation for the man would have to choose to do things that would seem not of Me and I am saying the word seems here. According to his knowledge of Me he would have to make decisions that would not necessarily be saintly. So I chose a man who did not know what you know and you foolish people expect him to be a saint when in reality he is one compared to all the evil around both you and him.

But his judgment is not in your hands it is in Mine and he was created by Me to be used by me and he pleases Me in his choices of policy on many, many things. Still, you dare play with those who you know do wickedness. I will visit this sin. Read in the Word how many times I warned the people before I moved upon them. Before they forced me to come upon them and deal with them so sharply there would be no mistake that I AM GOD! Remember I AM according to My word a terrible God when I am moved out of My place. Like a Father fed up with children not listening I will personally take care of it.

You are a people who thought that you were doing My will and yet never worked out your own salvation with fear and trembling. And because of that, you can't hear Me. I don't intend for that day to come to any of My children where they have to be lost, I desire to deal with them today, for today is the day of salvation. Right now is the hour to begin to realize that when you gave your life to Jesus, you never got everything under His blood. Had you done so, all those things that you let slide by, all those things that you have permitted to think that we're going to be alright with Me would have never followed you to this hour and forwarding to the judgment. This is a presumptuous sin. I heard those who called themselves my prophets and pastors and apostles (which is really outrageous because so many lifted up to the highest and do such wrong in private and they know it) and I did not call them. I have heard them say "It's going to be alright; God will take care of it." I hand your sin right back to you over and over for you to deal with and get it right with Jesus enough to get it under the blood of Jesus and you throw it right back at Me because you believe the lies of those leaders.

Some of you came out of deep sin. And yes, I cleansed you and even delivered you. And the moment you entered into your new life, presumed you that all of those tendencies that you had fallen into, things that you had done were gone. You went to an altar of prayer and said a sinner's prayer, and never did you go on to a personal journey with Me to work them all out. If salvation was not to be worked out, then how can I truly turn your life around? The roots that took a lifetime to grow in this world needed to die. And some of you never touched the surface. You turned around yes, and faced your past life, but instead of working it out with Me, you thought now I am free and every person that ever touched my life sins and will answer to God. Or you thought now I am righteous and holy and whoever dares question that will answer to God.

And suddenly and as quickly as that, you had become stillborn. For instead of asking Me to forgive others, you cursed them and in so doing you cursed yourself. Only this time, you claim to know something that you know nothing about. You strove to keep your forgiveness but forgot where you began not to forgive. It comes and visits over and over and you don't realize it is following you until you do something about it. How can you instantly change without getting into the Word? How can you take just a part of the Word and claim everything good for you in the Word without getting rid of all of the things that are wrong in you? I intended for you to bring every thought into captivity of Christ. I will tell you how you can. By using the word as a horoscope for comfort and foretelling the future for fun but never to truly repent and change your evil ways and seek to know Me. So then you are susceptible to every trick of Hollywood, sports, and devils who know the truth; tremble but never change. You in this condition become the enemy's tool in church, at home everywhere and even in your finances as you support those who are not of Me.

How do you bring every thought into captivity to Christ? I heard a young preacher say that it was impossible to do so. He also said that if your sin manifests before you in a service that you are to ignore it or never claim it; that it is not yours. He doesn't know what he is talking about because he never took that journey with Me to work out his own salvation. When it comes up before you in a service it is because all things are manifest in My sight. It manifests so that you can seek Me and find out why it came to you. Is it a curse from others, a curse from Me that you can't get rid of until you talk to Me how to be rid of it. Or is it something that you suppressed but never was rid of? These kinds of preachers have knowledge of certain things and they actually entertain you with their props of making the covenant seem real when they don't know what their covenant is. Having knowledge puffs up. They know how to talk about it but not how to live it for if he did he never would have taught to suppress the Holy Spirit conviction in the service. Quenching My Spirit is very real. Frustrating My Spirit is very real also.

Every night this vessel would write down everything that she could remember what happened that day and take it before me. She would write what she remembered and ask Me to line her up to My understanding. And I would through this reveal to her all the things that hindered her from being close enough to Me and why and where. There is much, much more to this teaching but I will not reveal it in a book. It needs to be taught to those who claim they know it all but I refuse to give freely that which is holy between her and I to those who only want to use it for self-recognition and self-gain.

I assure you it took a lot of time that none of you were willing to take. Each day her mistakes etc. became smaller and smaller until one day all that was from her memories, her past doings were gone and put under the blood of My Son Jesus Christ and healed as she prayed for Jesus to save her from it all. I did this for her because I knew that I could trust her that when we got done she would never lift herself up so high that she was above others because they did not know the what she knew. She treats every soul the way Paul the Apostle did. She values them as someone that I the LORD loved so much I died for them. Do you value them? Do you honestly believe that if you copy this with an insincere heart that I would lead you like her? Think again because real power I NEVER release to those who want to play.

None of this is meant to be used by those who would use you and abuse you. It is written for My church; treatment of My children among themselves. The soulless who does not want Me I will judge so be kind, generous and love the brethren. But stay away from those who claim My Son's name and blaspheme Him. The world is different they don't know what you know therefore you can't separate from some because many are the needs of your life to go out with them. Even then make sure you are holy, righteous in Christ and true before you dare make any judgments on another. My word says judge nothing until the LORD comes. I was not talking about His second coming. I was talking about coming upon the situation or need. Anything in this word that you think applies for you to know what is in the heart of any man think again. For if they belong to Me then I keep the secrets of their hearts hidden between Me and them. But if they are willfully and deliberately sinning according to their knowledge then it is exposed to all without having to do one thing. Most of the time you see what and who you are and claim it is Me who revealed it. I don't tell them your secrets that you share with Me why would I tell you theirs. The only way I reveal anything like that is if it is the only way to save them and you are not the judge of that even though you have set yourself so high and mind everyone else's business.

Some of you kneel at an altar of prayer and pray by asking God to come into your heart. And because you set yourself so high, higher than God intended you to be, you begin to judge everybody and everything. And in so doing you bring judgment upon your own selves...

Some of you seek God for a while, start out correctly and soon become what you used to be, heady, high-minded, selfish only now you seem to have power with Me. Some because I gifted you do not realize that the gift is not proof that your heart is right with Me. The evidence of the fruits within your personal life between you and Me is evidence of who you are. I call many but few are chosen and this means that although I called many few are obedient. Do you honestly think that I Am with a man who made himself king through selling My Son's Words and insults those who don't know what he knows? Would I act that way? Would I laugh and mock them because they don't know what I know and call them stupid? Did I not say in James that I give to every man freely and upbraid him not? He comes to Me and asks me for wisdom I give it if he will receive it so why do you constantly mock people for not having this great wisdom you think you have? You say you have no respect for anyone who will take abuse yet you abuse My children.

Some of you desire so much to be seen that you sit so high and I cannot even begin to put you where you belong for you refuse to go. You keep blaming the devil for all the things that you brought upon yourself by not hearing Me. The devil laughs in your face and My heart is broken because you have given the enemy so much power over your life. The devil in your life is only as powerful as you give him what belongs to Me. You want the signs, you want the miracles, but you refuse to go where every Christian must go and that is on a journey to work out every root that caused you to fall. I designed it so that you will never fall. And because the journey is not easy, because it is not glorious, and because it seems to take away from you as you die to self, you get rebellious and refuse to go and do as I called you to do. Only you cover it all up and refuse to face yourself as you are. So many of you strove to be higher than anyone else and when you see someone that you are afraid has more than you; you make sure you pull them down. Don't you know that is the action of witches who refuse to allow anyone to be higher than them? This lust to be the leader above everyone else has been given to you because as you wanted this responsibility never thinking what it meant I gave it and now You are now responsible for things that you don't even know you did wrong. And you will answer for them. Why? I warned you in the Word not to desire to be a leader because the responsibility is so great. It is impossible for man to count how many people get into this so they can be seen, heard and understood. It is like a child rushing to a something to get attention. That is part of the cleansing out of the self that wasn't done first. So many of you took it as a call from Me to get into ministry. How many women just up and left their homes and families and said the LORD called them into ministry? How many men did the same thing? How many deserted what they had a responsibility for and blamed Me and claimed I called them out of it? How many children are deserted and not properly taken care of like the mother who claimed she was called to be a pastor. And she would belittle her precious well behaved little girl and emotionally beat her with verbal words. They will ring in her ears. "You're not going to embarrass me in front of the whole church!" Those were cruel, mean, rotten words spoken to a 12-year-old girl who said and did nothing back. Who mentally and emotionally was so abused that she wouldn't stand up because she did believe the word to honor her mother even if she didn't deserve it. Children remember they don't forget. Get a good picture of what I see when you do these things. Fortunately for the church, this woman lost her license. Her girlfriends still support her, still hold her up and esteem her. Where is common sense???

Look at you! listen to your own heart right now as you read! You think "How dare she touch me I am God's anointed?" if she touched you then she should be afraid but if I touched you then you need to be afraid and repent.

Matthew 3:12 'He will burn up the chaff with unquenchable fire.' How does Jesus do that? With My Word telling you that I Am a consuming fire, how hard could that be to understand? What do you think it means to be baptized with fire? Do you just skip over those scriptures because they are too hard to understand for you? Do you picture Me as a person such as yourself that surely I did not mean fire? Surely I did not mean consume. Did I? What did I mean then if I did not mean fire? When you feel the heat of My Spirit upon you I have come for two things only; to burn out sin or to destroy the works of the flesh in you so much there might not be anything left.

You can understand that you can burn with passion, you can burn with lust. Both can consume your whole beings. You can burn with anger, you can burn with hate, and you can burn with compassion, you can burn with love. And you can burn with Me for I AM a consuming fire. As the disciples said when Jesus talked to them 'did not our hearts burn within us?' Would you not rather suffer your works to be burned here and not go to hell? Would you not rather endure hardship here and not in eternity? The scriptures that deal with fire should be the ones that you first work with, and help Me do an operation within your heart and mind that you will never fall."

Understand one thing that if the motives of your heart are not right you will think you follow instructions here and not do so because you need your heart cleansed from wanting to be higher and better than anyone else or lusting for importance, lusting for more, lusting to be seen, lusting to be understood etc. In the back door comes sexual lust for lust is so greedy within you lusting for bigger churches or more money consumes you. And you never notice or recognize that back door. And until you address the front door the back door will ALWAYS remain open.

PART V

THE FEAR OF THE LORD IS THE BEGINNING OF WISDOM: IT IS REVERENCE

"knowing the terror of the Lord, we persuade men; but we are made manifest unto God and I trust also are made manifest in your consciences." (II Corinthians 5:11)

DO YOU TRULY understand what the fear of God is before your eyes? Do you know that when you have the fear of God to guide you that you will ALLOW yourself to be led by God to not do certain things enabling you to hear His voice? Jesus knocks at the door of your heart. He doesn't kick it down. He wants your respect, reverence that some say is fear. But it is a Godly fear that knows that I AM GOD! Human nature will play games with anyone who permits them to do so but I don't give you special dispensation of the gospel to do the things you have been doing. You presume too much and take those things upon yourselves. Then My Word, My Son gets the blame.

I will begin with telling you about when I visited and called this vessel to write her first book. It was April 2002. She was worshipping me when the presence of My Holy Spirit began to pour upon her in massive waves of favor. She fell to her knees and basked in My Presence. She had no idea of why I was pouring out My Spirit upon her. I wanted to touch her and reach her in such a way that I knew she would be able to completely accept Me without doubt, without fear of mistakes, without having to try the spirits. So I revealed to her My Glory. To her, My Presence began to intensify until

I was all-consuming and all-powerful. And she trembled within My fear with every atom of her being. And within herself, she wondered why she wasn't dead. When I subsided just a little, she asked Me, 'Why am I not dead?' I told her, 'You are no different than any other of My Prophets for they have all said 'Woe is me, I am undone, for I have seen God and what man has seen God and lived?'

To her, she could see Me right in the middle of all My glory, as Moses saw Me in the burning bush. She saw Me and heard Me speak a message to her and these were the words that I spoke. 'I want you to write a book. I appeared to you this way because I have a message to those who call themselves my prophets. This book will be entitled "Knowing the Terror of the Lord" Below the title she could see (we persuade all men II Corinthians 5:11). "The first message must be to those who call themselves My Prophets. Ask them this question, 'Are you able to stand in My Presence with the glory of My Spirit and live?' I revealed to her that I wanted it to be made known that there are those who think that they are My prophets and they are destroying My Prophets and they think they are doing Me a favor. This book is to being written to warn every person who will not take heed to My warnings; that I will visit them the way I did her and will they endure the touch?

We will go back in time and I will describe My first visit to her. Many years ago when she was very young as a Christian, she was home all alone. She lived farther out in the country and her husband was not home. It was about three o-clocks in the morning and someone knocked at the door. By this time in her life, Satan had bombarded her repeatedly, and she knew when an evil spirit was present. She knew so little about how to protect herself from Satan and I wanted to reveal to her My Power and Presence in such a real way that there would be no doubt as to Who I Am. A young man appeared out of nowhere and asked if he could come in and use the telephone. She answered 'No' and as she turned away from the door she felt an evil presence sweep through the room from him. To her, it was the most powerful presence of that kind that she had ever felt before and before she could become frightened. I immediately stood before her as an angel. And all that had tried to enter her home in one moment had disappeared. I spoke and said 'You think that is powerful then feel this!' She was so small before Me and she immediately fell to her knees, and she bent over with her head buried in her lap. She had her eyes covered with her arms and even though her head was buried she could still see Me plainly as though she was still looking up. With her eyes still closed she could see the sword in My hand as I raised it above her. In seeing all this above her she knew she was powerless to move or think to prevent Me. And I swung My sword full force through her body and she could feel what it felt like to die physically without being dead and what it felt like to die spiritually without being dead and she trembled. When I say what it felt like to be dead spiritually I am speaking about the way Ananias and Sepphira felt when they fell over dead for lying to the Holy Spirit in the Apostles. Acts 5:10 10 Then fell she down straightway at his feet, and yielded up the ghost: and the young men came in, and found her dead and, carrying her forth, buried her by her husband.

My main purpose for the whole visit was to reveal to her not to ever be afraid of anyone or anything that comes from people or from Satan. And from that day on she obeyed Me. She had become afraid of no one except Me (the Lord). She went and did all that I asked her to do and still does without any fear of any man or anything but I the Lord. Please do not puff yourselves up as to believe that I would destroy anyone that touches you during the time that you play your games with Me. Please do not think for one moment that you are able to send destroying angels. All too often those that claim to be Mine, which claims that I will take care of their enemies, cannot see that all along what they have been doing is as bad as their enemies. I said I stand at the church, I defend it, and I will destroy the enemies of the Holy Spirit. Many of you who claim My name is still My enemy, and your church is not defended by Me. I will defend every church of Mine from being destroyed. If your church is destroyed ask yourself a question where is your disobedience? Search that out so you will be able to repent. I Am faithful in My Presence to every church. Not because the pastor is anything, and not because the people are anything, but because I Am God and I promised in My Word that I would be faithful.

In order to deliver this message, My prophet had to endure the terror of Me repeatedly. She would lay before Me for hours. Suspended in My time which is the here and the now; where there is no tomorrow, no yesterday, only now. To her she was not on the floor; she was somewhere in time. Because I called her out of time and all around her was nothingness. All she felt or knew was a tremendous awareness of right now that I the Lord was deciding if I was going to cast her away from My Presence forever.

Now, listen to what I Am saying here. I did not say that I was considering casting her away. I said that she felt as though I was considering casting her away. And I let her think that so that she would know what it felt like, so that she could come out of it, and tell it to warn those who do not believe 'that it is a fearful thing to fall into the hands of the Living God' as written in Hebrews 10:13. I have given the experience of visiting hell to some to have them come back and tell it. I have given them the experience to visit heaven to come back and tell it. This one I have visited with My glory that she may come out of it and she may tell it.

She laid in My Presence for hours and My Presence touched every atom of her being. She was unable to form one thought. All she had was a total awareness of the presence of My Spirit, and of My being on the verge of making a decision concerning her soul. She could feel the 'now' of it, that in one second, in one moment; a decision was being made for all eternity concerning not only her life but her spirit. And she was powerless to lift one finger, or say one word, to do one thing to affect or change My decision. There was no defense, no excuse that could come to mind. No remembrance of knowledge of anything that she had ever said or done, for that was past and this is the now. The only way that it could be explained to you, and it is not her explanation, is when you meet Me, there is no such thing as remembering anything to utter an excuse because I hold all the memories; I hold all of the things needed for that decision in that day, not you. My, how you have puffed yourselves up to actually believe that you will be able to speak or remember in My Presence. Your choices and abilities end here when it comes to excuses. For in rejecting the truth here there are no excuses.

I describe it plainly in Psalm 1 that the ungodly will not stand at the judgment. The ungodly are not like the sinner who knows nothing. They are the opposite of Godly because they know better and refuse to repent. This is why it is very important to read the Bible to be able to see yourselves as I see you, not as you gloss over anything to be. Yes, it is very much like a courtroom. And yes the books will be opened. But while they are opening you will not have the opportunity to plead your case. Here on earth, an evil lawyer can plead a case for a reasonable doubt. But up here with Me, there is no such thing as being able to prove or plead a reasonable doubt for some of you. Your case is being pled here and now as you reason with Me, in prayer. And since you have been given every chance here and did not use it; in eternity you have just run out of chances. Read My Word. If any man tells you differently and you choose to believe what they have taught you and not what I taught in My Word that was simply your choice. All choices have consequences, some to the good and some to the bad.

Terrorized by My Presence so completely she endured and endured and endured. She could actually feel that she would be gone forever in one second, unable to ever change the decision forming in My mind. When I finally released her she asked Me why she went through that. And I gave her a word of knowledge and I said 'passion'. Her passion for Me burned so hotly, that she was willing to endure anything, suffer anything if only she could please Me. She went through the stages of thinking that she could please Me with all the things that she did for Me or the church. She discovered that there was only one way to please Me and it is written in Hebrews chapter eleven. That one way is to believe on My Son Jesus Christ with all her heart to believe that He loved her so much that He died for her. To believe that He is God and that He resurrected from the grave to prove there is life after death. And for us to be a shining living example that in Jesus we also can rise from the dead and get into heaven through His blood. This is all she ever desired, was My will. This was only one touch of My Spirit and My glory. And it was done to make it real to not only her but to you that I Am the Lord and there is no other. To make it so real that I do cast souls into outer darkness, away from My Presence. That I do make decisions as to what I am going to do and no one, I repeat no one will be able to say one word, give one excuse. In that day I will do according to every man's works in Me

I did make a decision that very day. I decided how I was going to eventually use her. During that time she had a tumor below her left breast and she was exhausted from the experience, so much so that she fell fast asleep. As she slept, I put My hand inside of her and held the tumor in my hand and squeezed it. I dissolved it the way I put My hand in Adam's body as he slept and took out his rib to make Eve. In her sleep, she felt the pain of My hand crushing it and when she woke up it was completely gone. She never asked Me to heal it, just like she never asked Me to heal her of cancer. She asked Me after being told she was definitely going to die and in around two weeks and she cried out to Me. She said "Live or die; I don't care as long as I Am obedient and do Your will. For in that I know that I will be pleasing to You." All she ever wanted was to be with Me. That is love, and even I marveled at it. A few years ago she was becoming very upset. She seemed to lose the joy and was troubled. She came to Me daily with it and I told her that the only problem she was having was she hated this life so much and longed to be with Me. But that I could not take her yet because I planned on using her. She was so filled with love for Me and We were so close that I stopped her and told her to back up and say nothing more. Think nothing more; just stop altogether and tomorrow I would tell her why. She obeyed Me and the next day I told her it was because of one more step closer to Me and she would have been no more. She would have been just gone with Me into heaven. Like some say Enoch went.

This is what I hope through this book to spring forth in you. She cried constantly to do My will, even if she had to die and many times she almost did. Her spirit during that time would just slip away and with My hand, I held it within her body. Sometimes her body was so weak, that her heart could not take the strain and she would just slip away ever so softly, and I ever so gently held her within My great hand.

If only you could find it in your heart to be like Jesus in her and take your hands off of the controls of your life and die daily. Because tears endure for a night but joy does come in the morning. That light that was to shine in you, you being the person reading this book, that light was ever so slowly snuffed out. Lying to yourself, took you to only one place, one course, one road; repentance. What you never truly did the first time, no matter who you know, or where you go, until you help Me to do the first works and bring Me meat worthy of repentance, you will remain self-deceived until it is too late. Because you have known I was there from the time you were little doesn't mean that you did what I wanted you to do within My Word. It only means that I called you and you went your own way in religion, not in My Word. Because you had some knowledge of Me and My Word for years ahead of those that you do know, means nothing to Me.

It is what you did with it, not by making excuses that you do not act according to the Word because God is still working on you. The true answer is, to back up and admit you are wrong and that you are like everyone else, you have to get on your knees and ask for forgiveness and to be led to repentance. What a silly person you are to think that I Am with you when you dare speak constantly that you know, you know, and you never humble yourself before Me in someone who does behave themselves properly. How long do I have to suffer your years of claiming that you are Mine and you know, but you have no true humility? Accountability, responsibility, and much more get thrown out the window when you see yourself as perfect before you permit Me through the Word to perfect you.

This is one of the reasons why for this time, for this hour, My hand is writing this book in the hopes that there will be some of you who will be willing to see yourself as you really are. No matter how high you sit, no matter how long you have sat there, no matter how many people supposedly love and respect you, no matter how much you believe or think you have; you need to examine yourself today. For today is the day of salvation. This is the now. Look around you. Is there any place that is a promised security on life that you will not have to face Me and soon? I say look around you because if you do, you will see that no one has any guarantee of a tomorrow, not even as you know it (meaning your quality of life financially and physically) not being taken away from you. I wrote this in 2006 and prosperity for many of my children enjoyed the blessing. By 2008 the same people who had a beautiful home lovely children, the best clothes, a nice car. They were now out in the street living out of their cars standing in church food bank lines and getting the benefit of second-hand clothes that some people gave them. Where My children went for prosperity and refused to believe that they needed to die to self they now had to die to all that they wanted or needed. Now they have a chance to see me as I really Am.

A short while ago, I came to her again. She did something that all of you take so lightly; therefore I will not tell you what it is, lest you judge her. Right in the middle of it, My Glory appeared and she knew that any second she could be gone forever. I told her 'Do you not know that right now at this exact moment, I could take you out and cast you away from My presence for all eternity?' She was getting into the vehicle with her husband at the time and she turned to look at him to see if he could feel what she felt. And I said 'I could make it look like a heart attack or anything that

I so desire, but believe Me, I will take you if you continue.' This was the harshest that I have ever been to her and she cried out because of the reality of Who I Am. I was so real to her that she could not bring herself to want to breathe for the next couple of seconds. She could see clearly that she could not live without My Presence so much that she was like a baby feeling for every step in every second of her life. Get this picture in your mind; what she could not bear was her knowing that she would be without My Spirit, My Presence for even a moment, let alone facing that reality for eternity. Crying out to Me she did not want to live any longer if she would repeat the same mistake and come to this very same place. She begged Me to take her life. And I settled her down and gave her the blessing of My Spirit and she once again basked in My Presence and was comforted by Me and Me alone. Do the words like 'castaway' or 'outer darkness' mean anything to you? Does that ring a bell? Perhaps as we continue it will occur to some of you how important it is not to leave a calling that I have called you to, and place yourself where you don't belong.

Please, for your sake don't be deceived into believing that she sinned so badly that I dealt with her so harshly because the only reason she endured these things was to tell it. I wanted to make it real to you through her testimony that I Am God. In Luke 13:2-5 "And Jesus answering said unto them, Suppose ye that these Galileans were sinners above all the Galileans because they suffered such things? I tell you, Nay; but except ye repent ye shall likewise perish. Or those eighteen, upon whom the tower of Siloam fell, and slew them, think ye that they were sinners above all men that dwelt in Jerusalem? I tell you, nay; but, except ye repent, ye shall all likewise perish.' I spoke in Isaiah 43 that I called you to be My witnesses that I Am God.

When I healed her, I put a song within her, to make it real, to tell how I saw the whole situation, to tell what I wanted her to see, that she may be able to tell it to you. 'Mine eyes have seen the glory of the coming of the Lord; He hath trampled out the vintage where the grapes of wrath are stored. He hath loosed the faithful lightening of His terrible swift sword; His truth is marching on, glory, glory Halleluiah, glory, glory, Halleluiah.' Can you see it? Can you see what I am saying to you? The lightning of the Word of God penetrated within her HEART down to the bone and the marrow of her being; that is where the grapes of wrath are stored in the heart. God hates the sin that is cultivated by the heart to make all of His commandments vain. He trampled them out with His faithful terrible swift sword. For in the moment that I came in My Glory, I revealed to her, her sin against the Word. Listen please, I appeal to you, it is real.

If you think for one moment in anything that you have read that you would have done a better job than her, or would not have done the things she did, I am telling you the truth, repent, because you are the one who is so much worse off than she has ever been. Listen, carefully I Am going to visit everyone who claims to be Mine in this manner. and get it right down into your ears. Her eyes have seen the glory of the coming of the LORD. If they are where they ought to be then they will be filled with joy and blessing, but if they are self-deceived they can and will wish that they never forced My hand within them. Listen to what I say. Within them, the Holy Spirit within you. I will touch you and it will not be a blessing to your flesh if you lie to me. If you continue in your lie of claiming I Am with you or called you to be something that I never called you to. You will know in that day that I Am God! But I Am merciful also and will give you the opportunity to repent before I come. So do it now, for today is the day of salvation.

And if you turn this in your head and your heart to say this can't be God, for it is threatening. Remember this one thing. If this is a man's message it would be a threat. But since it is directly from Me, it is a warning. A warning that is designed to lead you to repentance and to ask for forgiveness and work it all out with Me. Psalm 51:4 'Against Thee, Thee, only, have I sinned, and done this evil in Thy sight: that Thou mightest be justified when Thou speakest, and be clear when Thou judgest.' This vessel has nothing to do with what I Am saying; as a matter of fact, she would never write a single word unless she knows that I said those words.

The last visit was not that difficult for her to endure. She could feel in My Spirit that it was I and she could feel My terrorizing presence, but she could also feel that it felt good to her. Because now she was so close to Me, that when I come and visit; the flesh isn't reigning and is not in control enough to be terrorized. The Spirit rules and reigns completely and we have sweet fellowship together and I use this Presence as a way to let her know that I Am the same God who has power over life and death, over heaven and hell, overall that she is and all that she will be, and she has a peace that was borne out of the most comforting love that any person could have with an awesome God. Many times as she is writing and doubt would come to her as she to really write this? And I would allow her to feel My terrorizing presence, not harshly but enough that I could speak through My glory as a reminder and ask her this gently 'How could you doubt?'

After the first visit where she laid for hours, she then begged Me over and over and over to never touch her again like that. Then as she grew in Me, she began to realize what that visit did, it changed something within her. She realized how it changed her and gave her the power to do and overcome things that she took so lightly before. And she began to pray for Me to come again just like that and help her to be where she needs to be. Knowing how traumatic it was for her in the physical she still desired to be close to Me and I answered her cry. Now, no longer does she beg Me to not come to her that way. She prays if I need it, I need it, please come to Lord.

Last year, she laid her head on her pillow to retire for the night. Suddenly the terrorizing Presence of Mine came right out from within her being. This Presence she knows so well. The Presence of MY Glory came right out of her heart. I intensified quickly and immediately and by the time she could ask Me what was going on, why did she experience this? I said 'I wanted you to know the power within you' I revealed to her that the power within her was equal to the power that the apostles had when Ananias and Sepphira lied to the Holy Spirit within them and paid for it. Are you lying to Me and thinking all is well with your soul? Make it right today, now. For today is the day of salvation. There is nothing that is able to separate you from My love. Romans 8:38, 39 'for I am persuaded that neither death nor life, nor angels, nor principalities, nor powers, nor things present, nor things to come. Nor height nor depth, nor any other creature shall be able to separate us from the love that is in Christ Jesus our Lord. No angel can separate you, no one can separate you. The only person who can is you. By choice, by the rejection of the truth, or reception of the lie because only the truth will set you free. Every soul that has My Holy Spirit indwelling and every day of their lives they reject Me, and cause Me to dwell where they take Me. And they do this without the fear of Me that they need to benefit their soul. There is no fear of God before their eyes making them capable of anything in My name.

Many of you thus far have taken all this so lightly. It is a very important hour upon the church right now, and the only way you are safe is to be safe in the arms of Jesus through the power of His Word guided by My Holy Spirit. Dangerous times are coming. I the LORD was revealing to her that many were going to lose all they had and be invaded. As you protect one door another tries to open and you must, more than ever before, run to the Only One who loves you. But another danger lurks, and you may not believe what is about to be written, and I am going to reveal the truth in My Word, why it is so important to know how to possess your vessel and how to make sure you are obeying the Word. Because surely in an hour you think not the Son will come and He will bring His reward with Him. And for those of you who value Him in your soul, it will be a day of complete joy that no man can take away. And to ensure that moment take heed to what is written

Your opinion of Me means nothing to Me at all. I will put it this way, what she went through with Me is a warning to all of My prophets of how I most definitely will visit those who need to be corrected. O man or woman of God prophecy is not written in stone it works according to the heart and mind of those who are spoken over. If they repent I change My mind towards them. If they do not I change in another direction. When certain bad things are told to warn or rebuke it is to waken you and the people up. That all may benefit but the heart of My people can be changed from the leaders on down so none be destroyed. I Am here to protect you NOT harm you. Prophecy is never to be given strictly for comfort. Prophecy is for warning My people to turn from their wicked ways. It is also for prayer first. That plea to turn from your ways and follow Mine is the greatest call of love that there is. And some of you pray alright, but you pray for what you believe is the prophecy and for it to be fulfilled. So that you are not found to be mistaken, you pray for it to come true. You never realize that you could be deluded through the flesh. When I reveal something to you about any individual, let alone anyone famous it is not necessarily to tell everyone. It is first for prayer. Not a prayer to bring it to pass. Prophecy is for warnings, to rebuke and exhort so that people could have an opportunity to repent before I come before it is too late. No prophet is a prophet without the ability to warn. Comfort to those who like or support you is not true prophecy. Sometimes I do comfort and I do use My prophets for that. But I have some who don't believe in telling the truth. They see it, they feel it, but they just don't speak it out of fear. And that fear can cause them to take on the wrong thing at the wrong time and all the while they will think it is Me. A prophet has no power to give you a prophecy as though it comes from him or her. They are only for confirmation to what I spoke into your spirit in the first place.

Some go from church to church to have a prophet pray over them or speak over them and many times none of it comes true because you won't go where I called you to go. You won't do what I called you to do in order to bring anything to pass. But if a man or a woman speaks to you about something I NEVER spoke to you about then they are not telling the truth; because I will always confirm My Words. And when you pray in tongues by yourself do you ever get interpretation? This vessel prays then waits and I reveal to her what she prayed for. The only time I don't tell it all to her is if it concerns someone else's heart and it is none of anyone's business. I Am speaking to prophets now a word for a person is for you to pray, and to tell them the truth. It is for you to reveal it to them and give them an opportunity to change it through forgiveness and repentance.

I choose who I use, and so many times you get it all mixed up in your minds here on earth. As though you earned something through the things you go through. Yes, you earn some things, but you never earn the calling that comes straight from My Throne to belong to Jesus, you never earn the calling of a prophet. Nor can you become a prophet by the laying on of hands. Nor can you earn being a prophet or an apostle because of anything. I call them. Whoever tells you that may not be deliberately lying but they are not telling you the truth. They can impart who and what they are in you but I assure you that prophetic utterance does not a prophet make. And because they wrote a book or poured oil all over your head did not make them anything in My sight. I watched too many of My called children wasting their life patterning themselves after these self-seeking wicked men. If I were not the LORD I would be outraged that many pastors invite these people to speak in their churches and they do not know what they are talking about.

The Charismatic movement had a great outpouring of the Holy Spirit years ago. And like so many today when My Spirit comes upon a service they still do not know truly why I, My Holy Spirit has come. It is to draw you into the Word. Into loving My Son in His word the way this vessel writing this book did. It is to cause you to do the first works of working out your salvation with fear and trembling. But many of you went into the Word to find out how to use Me. How to use My Word, how to use Me to build your churches. Anyone who goes into My word will come out with many aspects of Me and they will have more knowledge and understanding in certain things that will make them look like they are called. It would have been better for them to fall upon their knees and seek My Son and the truth in His word instead of leading generations into error. That is why you have pastors who can write a book and them not be of Me at all. Go to their services and they teach on one word that is out of the dictionary to prove how intelligent they are and they are offended when you don't remember how bright they think they are. They are an offense to Me being in authority that they misuse and do not understand making slaves out of their congregations to build them up.

To be a prophet is a calling, and that calling has a great price on it. I chose you, you did not choose Me. I know it has been said repeatedly, and you think that you know what I Am saying. But I tell you even now you do not know, because had you known you would have dug deeper and gotten closer and would not reject the truth. You would not have rejected this book. It is kin to the Bible and it has all the attributes of the Bible in being Holy Spirit inspired. Are you truly Holy Spirit inspired? Because if you are not, what you seem to be, what you seem to have will fade away, and as you see it take flight to repent and pray that you do not lose it all. It is in the word for a reason there comes a time that the I visit and when I do I take everything you think you have off of you. I take it I tell you. I just lift it; because what will remain is Me in you. And if you in the depth of your own mind and teachers forced Me (at least to your beliefs or your thinking because you can't force Me into anything); if you did it by repetition, or by fasting and praying as though the number of weeks you seemed to spend with Me or the times you gave up one or two things for a season I AM laughing right not at the puniness of your beliefs. Because I see the day I appointed to visit you. I see that when I do you will be devastated and gasping for life. I don't care how long you seem to have served Me. I don't care how long you seemed to have saved souls. If

Mexico is an example of your saving souls I tell you right now there is no salvation there thanks to you.

I AM not saying all and if you dare to quote Me as though I apply all these words to everyone but you... Think again This vessel writing this book did not pray for this, nor did she ask for this and even now as she writes this is not something that she asks Me to fulfill. She doesn't have to. Our relationship is unlike yours and so many others. She never has to ask Me to fulfill the Words that I give her. She doesn't spend her time asking Me to do anything that she may have believed, understood, or known. She knows that if I want that, she will have it if it is I that speaks it will come to pass. So she makes it her business to be sure that it is I that speaks. She rests the way all of you need to rest. I Am not speaking about your special little combinations of turning My Word to be used to suit your need. You treat Me as though I Am somebody that you carry in your back pocket and you pull out Me when you need a parking spot or want help in doing your filthy evil. I AM not there only you are.

Listen to what I Am saying to you. When you as a prophet are where you need to be with Me, dead to self, dead to all that you think or feel, then I truly dwell within you and that releases Me as I Am. There is no need to ask for it is already clearly yours. As you read in this book how she expected Me to heal her. She did not ask, because her time of asking was over. She asked for the best things. She asked to be worthy of My gifts, to be honest, wise and filled with integrity even to the point of death. She asked for love no matter how she was insulted, even physically, mentally and emotionally hurt. Because she knew that is the way I loved her. She understood that is the way My Son loved her so much that He died for all of you.

She doesn't ever speak to Me as though I Am not there that I do not see, that I do not know, that I do not understand. Most of the time she communicates with Me, we both know who we are, and where we stand, and what is to be done. I sit across her table and sup with her. I am right in front of her always face to face. I never leave her nor forsake her and will always be with her like this even when she is called home. I, God the Father, I God the Son, and God the Holy Spirit will personally come for her and it won't be in sickness or disease. Nor will it be an accident or trouble of any kind. We will simply say "Come, it is time". And she will come to Us.

No, she is not perfect. Jesus asked many things because of those around Him. That they might believe. Jesus knew His relationship with Me and it was and as you know is very close. We as you well know are One; He communed with the Holy Spirit and (Myself God the Father) as One with Us, never as though He was separated asking for something. Now, if as a prophet you have this kind of relationship then you may take what she says and toss it behind you and pray for what you desire to have and expect Me to fulfill it. But if not, if this is not the kind of relationship that you have then you must be careful. For although I have said be careful for nothing in the Word, I have also said that you touch not Mine anointed. She completely understands the separation between the man, woman, their spirits, and My Spirit. She completely understands the gifts that I give to a man and a woman. She never fears where the separation is, she sees, she knows, and she understands because I have revealed it to her. The gift is not the man and the gift is not the woman, the gift is Me. Many of you still do not understand but as you read I will open your understanding up. You have confused My people that if they don't agree with you that they hate Me or are angry with Me. And in all your mistakes and misguided teachings you condemn them and use the Word against them and they feel it so much that some of them can't find the truth. So I raised up one that would tell the truth and I did this that she may speak to all of those who call themselves My prophets, not one, not two, not some, but all. And if you are one of them, then I tell you even now take heed, for I Am warning you. I Am correcting you, I Am calling you to come out from where you are and get into what I Am speaking about in this book for the time is at hand. My Word is to rebuke to exhort, it is for correction, it is for comfort, and it is for all things that need to be done in all things. The truth must be something that you completely trust to do the operation. She never doubts, believing always that the truth will do the operation. Because she knows that Jesus is the Truth. She trusts Him to do the operation. And when she stands before the man she doesn't mind their business although she has the power to see where everyone is at. Just like Jesus did not call out every demon everywhere He went for there were so many demons in the church of the day. He called out only the ones appointed for My purpose to accomplish My will even if none of you understand it.

In only your creatures were really preachers you would have seen that when you keep your eyes and heart focused on Me the enemy of your soul and your congregation would have had no power. But you feed his power as you play before Me.

Think what you want, but I gave this vessel Ezekiel, to say it whether they will hear or for bear. Many, who are not seen by the world claim to be a prophet and they are not and they destroy many of My true prophets because they are looking for their self-seeking purposes. And this needs to be read by them to warn them before I move. I give every soul a chance before I move.

Awake thou that sleepest and I will give thee light. This is the gospel; this is the truth and you need to hear as you have never heard before. This is the time this is the hour to let everything go. Those who have not died to themselves, who have not picked up their cross and followed Jesus will now have to die to themselves, they will now have to pick up their cross and follow the One they have claimed all this time. Now it becomes real. The words that are written here are life, when you receive them they breathe life into you. These words have the power to cause you to live. All that is mentioned in this book is to one purpose to cause you to see yourselves as you are, to cause you to turn away from where you have been and obey the Word now. I repeat Now! This section was written before the nation became more lawless by dumping Me out of this nation's laws and working hard to replace Me with another god and his laws.

Don't you realize what you have done when you threw your hands up in the air and refused to vote because you claimed they were all evil and when I came and brought you, someone, you then decided to listen to character assignation by the left and claimed you were vetting him? Do you have ANY idea when you voted for a party that supports abortion, supports godless ways and so much evil that I AM right there holding you accountable for listening to lies from the media who feeds character assignation and hatred? I revealed to My church PLAINLY that I do NOT support killing babies nor do I support many of the evil done. But I do support Israel; I do support you have the right to have protection by buying a gun. It says so In Luke how My Son Jesus told the disciples that they remembered the first time He told them to take nothing with them. But the second time He sent them out HE TOLD THEM TO SELL

ALL they had and BUY A SWORD. Because He KNEW that they were going to have to defend their homes and families. I Am not saying He told them to go to war, but He instructed them to be able and ready to protect themselves. It is a God-given right. But the enemy works hard in his children to take your guns so they can take over this nation. WAKE UP!!!! STOP supporting the evil claiming I Am leading you. You who do this without the fear of Me that they need to benefit their soul. There is no fear of God before their eyes making them capable of anything in My name.

Many of you thus far have taken all this so lightly. It is a very important hour upon the church right now, and the only way you are safe is to be safe in the arms of Jesus through the power of His Word guided by My Holy Spirit. Dangerous times are coming. I the LORD was revealing to her that many were going to lose all they had and be invaded. That was in 2007. This was written before the nation was turned upside down by it's infiltrated leaders and dumped Me out of the laws. As you protect one door another tries to open and you must, more than ever before, run to the Only One who loves you. But another danger lurks, and you may not believe what is about to be written, and I am going to reveal the truth in My Word, why it is so important to know how to possess your vessel and how to make sure you are obeying the Word. Because surely in an hour you think not My Son will come and He will bring His reward with Him. And for those of you who value Him in your soul, it will be a day of complete joy that no man can take away. And to ensure that moment take heed to what is written.

PART VI

THE DIFFERENCE BETWEEN AN ANTICHRIST AND THE MAN I CALLED

Who is a liar but he that denieth that Jesus is the Christ? He is an antichrist, that denieth the Father and the Son. (I John 2:22)

"OH, MY PEOPLE be not deceived! Because a man says he belongs to Christ saying he is a Christian and you know that he in other places claims to be another religion with another god, then he is the liar My word speaks about this. And in public, he says he is Christian and in private he worships another god. When you work for globalism you are working towards ushering in the true Antichrist who will not be revealed before the time. Do you know the difference between this kind of person and someone that I have sent to you for this nation that strives to bring this nation back to God?

A word to the prophets who could have made it easy for him but no, you had to try to control him. (I Am not speaking to every one of you, I am speaking to some of you) You had to pray to pull down what you didn't like about him when you needed to get your hands off of him and let him hear Me. The anointing that all those corrupt others rejected he strove to pick up and you troubled him in the Spirit because you wanted to control him the way you control the church and I promise you that if you don't repent in this kind of prayer you will answer to Me. Don't tell Me how you pray I know exactly how you think you control in your prayer closets. I know exactly how all of you pray. Don't you remember in the IRS scandal how the left wanted to know how the Republicans were paying? Don't you remember? I do, and they used it to defeat them.

When I say something to you and you accept it in your shallow understanding. You miss the mark when you grab it and run with it. Because there are things about situations that I strive to speak to you about, and you don't hear Me. Oh, it seems like you do, but you don't. And I will never lead any of my prophets to support anyone capable of destroying the helpless innocent individuals that cannot protect themselves. When you vote for anyone who supports abortion; not just late-term abortion where they crush the head and mutilate the bodies and sell them. But any abortion and you do this to keep a man who the media crucified when he actually has all his sins under the blood of Jesus which is none of your business. You are partaker of their evil deeds and you will answer for the same thing they do. Read Romans 2 you have pleasure in them who you know are worthy of death and you judge them so you will not escape judgment yourselves.

Listen to what I say. You said that once this person who wanted God to damn America was in office that everyone was to stand behind him and pray for him and help him to destroy this great nation. You who said these things lied on Me because you said I put him in office which I did not. It was YOU who wanted him by refusing to vote to lie that there was no good man to choose from. Lying that I would call a preacher into office and that is all that the enemy needed was someone he could make a fool out of and run roughshod over you. Because I said plainly the devil's children are wiser in evil than My children are because they focus on pleasing Me. You did not see that abortion is murder and you continued to support him. And the one right now who is against murdering babies you help others destroy. Where is your thinking?!! When you dare to listen to the media that feeds hatred of someone who wants to protect My children. Because medias own lives reek with evil doings that they have to keep their power over you and you let them. You let them, and I promise you to have a reward for it and when it comes; you won't be prepared for it. If they support people who love abortion enough to celebrate killing their babies their lives are filled with evil. If they support invading this country and call it immigration they are filled with self-purpose and lies. When they use women and children as human shields the way other terrorists do. You can be sure they are terrorists your letting in. Build that wall; save yourselves, your country, your children and your children's children. Those liars on television don't care if you live or die they just use you like they always did.

This is not a left book or a right book. This is a God book. This isn't what anyone else says about these things except Me. I have spoken about the things that I detest. I have spoken on the things that will hurt you if you continue to listen to a voice that hates my word enough to kick Me out. It is not conservative. It is My Son you are speaking about. He is holy and He made it clear what He wanted His church to be or do. Your leaders in the media, in the political world, in the church all deceived you. All you had to do is get on your knees and renounce every word that goes against My word. Every voice that is not of Me and asks Me to deliver you of the deception of devils. To bring you back into the truth and set you free and make a commitment to never vote another person in the office that supports the issues that I have told you are important to Me because they are important your life and your children's lives.

People who support this invasion have no idea that when those invaders are done they themselves will be destroyed for letting them in. You reap what you sow. If you don't care what happens to America's babies then you will pay a sacrifice of losing your babies.

Globalism will not save these people who help them get in here or get elected. These people have no loyalty to anyone or anything because they have no rule of law within them to tell them it is wrong to lie. They do all they can to get next to you to find your weaknesses and your leaders in the church are foolish enough to help them. Your church leaders forgot the Word that I taught them, that I will not share My Son's glory with any other god. That is real and it is something that I will hold you responsible for. The antichrist will destroy them all for in an hour that they will have to forcibly deny My Son Jesus Christ they will remember what it says in Revelations 13. Because the day is coming where people will have to lose their heads because they dared to play with devils and call themselves by My Name. Christian. Christ-like. No My friend that is not Christ-like. If you choose to deny Me now when it isn't so bad; how in the world are you going to resist denying Me then? And if you think they will let you live once you deny My Son. They will kill you anyway because they can never trust you because they have no trust. They have no soul that has right or wrong, good or bad, truth or lie they have permission to do every evil thing that I have taught in My word that I hate. And they all know their end and they know they are going to face Me and they lie and pretend thinking that I Am a man they can mess with. I AM GOD.

Don't you know the truth on the simple matters? So simple to see and hear and yet you turn over everything to stop a woman like this vessel from telling the truth and you help someone in office that would kill babies and claim Christianity. You dare to say even now there is no proof in the White House that any Christian is there. You who have millions of followers dare tell the nation such a lie! The very fact that they hate abortion, and stand for Israel was not enough for you??? How hard is your heart to obtain your will that you help others destroy the only one that I sent to bring this nation out of destruction that you helped to bring about by letting a person who brought this country to ruin with lawlessness? He knew what the Word said and he used it to turn this nation upside down by taking away the only thing that made this nation great. Me. The lawlessness began when they decided that they did not want God and guns like those on the right did. I, their hate they forgot they were rejecting Me. Oh, they changed it back someone feared enough to change it back but they never came back.

This is a plain and simple explanation between an antichrist spirit and one who hears the voice of the LORD for this nation. One worshipped another god and he sat under a pastor who damned America. And many of you big named preachers did the same thing but you didn't do it that way. You kept preaching America is going to pay. You betrayed your own nation when you should have been praying for it. Listen to what spirits you followed those that were not of Me. One stirred up racism and was worshipped by the lying controlling media. One tried to make a way for transgender which is a mental, emotional and physical torture to the children they are forcing this on. They are forcing a mental-emotional, physical torture that will scar them for years to come. And you supported him by telling your congregations that they must pray for their president because it was God who put him there? No, I did not put him there, you did!

I would never call anyone born in another country to lead anyone in this nation. Listen I would never call anyone to be a leader in this nation who wasn't born here; because in order to be President you have to be born here. You have to feel what an American Patriot feels. You have to know that a person born and raised from another country can never love this country. If they say they do they lie because they only intend to use it for their purpose of turning it into globalism? Don't you see this is why every true Patriot loves this President of 2018 they can feel his heart towards this nation they love him like he loves this nation? He is who he is; mistakes and all. He is an original American made created by God for this hour.

Oh, My people hear Me. You are on the brink of either having a few more years of Me in this country or you yourself bring in the Anti Christ and will have to lose your head to believe on Jesus Christ. Don't you see it up the road? Those people who lie to you they live, breathe and think there is no God. This is why the worst evil was done in the White House. It was so much worse than you heard; much worse than you know. And you have the gall to vet the only one who wants to stop abortion, stop the persecution of the Jews. I could go on and on but I don't need you to know exactly what I AM saying.

If a man or a woman gets their sins under the blood of Jesus Christ and they don't do what you are doing yet because you had the word for years and they have not. I did not and will not tangle him up in things that mean nothing. You do that. You let the one who needed to be dealt with and stopped go free. They laugh in My face and yours. They laugh because all their tricks and lies are right out in the open and no one does one thing about it. You want to know why You don't pray. You pray to put your hand on the innocent and control them. Ugh, is repulsive to Me.

It is not morally within the realm of a human being to make a decision to kill an innocent child and say that I Am with them. Therein is your key as to who you are listening to. I will not change My mind on crushing the heads of innocent babies or whatever other forms you develop to kill. A choice between a life and the baby's life is one thing. But not giving a woman who does not want the precious being growing within her the right to kill it; this is an atrocity, and to celebrate it in their meetings before the whole world is worse.

To vote because of a person's gender or because of their race is as close to stupid or insane. Or you vote for them because you are silly enough to like their looks or something to that effect is unbelievable. Do your own homework through a prayer asking Me to reveal the truth to you. But then I already revealed it in their fruits according to My word and you would not listen. And when I discover someone won't listen to Me I just don't bother to tell them anything anymore and they follow strong delusion because they did not love the truth, to begin with. I revealed to you this one and many of you won't listen. The two issues I brought forth are two of My main issues on the earth. For you, it is safe to vet every soul who comes into this country because many bring in another god and there is no blessing in your life for supporting such things. I am not telling you to go out and speak out against them. Nor am I telling you to go out and fight them or mistreat them. Some people are so violent you need to stay away from them whenever possible.

My Word plainly tells you that you will not hear My Son's voice crying in the streets about anything. I will never call any prophet from another country to go against My anointed ones here in the United States. Mine anointed know that I will never support anyone who believes there is a reason to destroy a helpless life; they know I do not operate like that. False prophets, false teachers, false preachers, and false media will all support these evils and if you call yourself by My name understand I AM nothing to play with. I will never call anyone in a few moments to make a judgment that I would support any person who believes that I am so evil that I would destroy and kill millions of innocents in this nation. I AM talking about children who are citizens, legally born here. Not someone who uses them to say they have a right to the birth here that they manipulated. So don't twist up these words it won't do you a bit of good. I am speaking about abortion here. And you should have known it I Am not speaking to any one individual, I Am speaking to many of you.

Because many of you plan to support people that think a woman has a right to choose and she does not! Only I do!!! I am speaking here about voting. About thinking you are taking on the lesser of two evils. There was one who claimed to be My prophet who said that no one should pray against abortion. That as soon as they did his congregation got sick because God put the evil in place and you weren't to touch it. So for years, My church listened to that. Never realizing that the enemy made them sick and they had power over it and over abortion.

The backlash of hell was so great no one wanted to face it. But this President faced it and he didn't know the things that you knew in the Word and you denied him. Many of you of the silent majority realized your sin and voted for him but many of you now are daring to turn because you spend too much time in entertainment; too much time in listening to opinions calling themselves news. Watching what is pleasant to the eyes. An hour after hour you do this until it contaminates your faith and you begin to turn on those things that mean more to Me than they ever did to you; because to you; your doctrines, churches, pastors, parties, games etc and Hollywood. All turned your head against My will. Repent! TODAY is the day of salvation.

I made a promise that I will take away what you seem to have if you do not use what I have given you. I have given you the power to discern in My Word. By their fruits, you will know them and if you support anyone that does these things and say that I Am with you, you then open the door to hurt yourself because I Am not a false prophet, I do n't change the truth into a lie. I do not take the truth and make it sound as though I Am righteous because I help someone destroy a child that I created. Life is in the blood. The blood of those children cries out the way Abel's blood cried out. You say it is a blob of nothing I say it is life. This was written during a time that no one was truly standing against abortion or when there were those who thought it was right to kill people. I always instructed to obey the law. When you do the ones who formed the laws are the ones who answer. But for years before this President, there was work to destroy the law in this country because it was of Me. Just like Mine anointed will be held responsible first. I will not begin to really deal with the world until I first deal with the church. The leaders of the church must endure my correction. If they dare say this vessel is the one saying this it is then between I and each one who holds themselves so high they can do anything in My Name.

It is one thing if a young person decides they want to go to war to defend their country and you find fault with that because you don't like war. But I give My children the power to defend their nation whether you like it or not. I put a noble cause within the heart of the young to lay down their life for their country without questioning that country. They have a love for it. It was born in them, and it was nurtured by Me. Whether you think it is a mistake or not, I give the power to do certain things. You say this country was deceived. I say to you right now that to stop an invasion of people wanting to come and destroy My people needs to be stopped.

Hear what I Am saying O My people, who call yourselves by My name. I hate no one. I hate the only sin. I Am against no one, I Am against sin. If you are committing it then I Am against you unless you repent. When you break from Mine anointed, (Mine Anointed is Jesus Christ) not some creature who claims to be a preacher even if I gifted him I will still turn him or her away if they don't repent. And you think I Am with you, it is described completely what I think about it in Psalm 2. Don't be mistaken the vessel's hand I Am using, is not saying this. These words are in My Word and its name is the Bible. And she is only typing what it says.

Some of My prophets who call themselves by My name are a disappointment to Me, for they don't know Me as they claim. Not all of them, but those who are shallow and think they are something. They support those who are capable of wicked things all because they look like they could be Mine, or they act like they could be Mine, I assure you, no one is Mine who can destroy the innocent. Not that I hate them, but that I simply Am not with their wicked works, and their success comes from those who support things that are not of Me. And that success and support will surely destroy them in the end if they don't repent. You're first innocent to protect are those who are born in this country and not through manipulation of the birth to steal a passage to invade.

I will say to you as written in Peter that there are those who make themselves willingly ignorant of one great fact. That the world was formed by the Word, and that the Bible sat in your home, or your parents home all of your life and never did you ever decide to sit down and read it. Your whole life passed by and you refused to read about My Son and what He said. Oh, I know you went to church faithfully. But you don't find salvation in Jesus Christ in a church that teaches another gospel and tells you that if you don't obey the church leaders, that you are not getting into heaven when they themselves won't obey the only leader and that is Jesus Christ, Who is the Word.

Read it in the gospel John chapter one, verse one. You never searched the scriptures to find Me. If there is anyone who tells you that if you do not follow their doctrine, their pastors, and their religion that you are going to hell if you avoid their gatherings because you found them to be liars. Remember they are cults. A cult's true meaning of the word is "where I AM not." When I send a messenger they are only that a messenger and you don't answer them you answer to Me.

Try as you might, you cannot get up above Me, nor can you get around Me. The belief that you will be able to stand before Me and that there will be one reason that you will be able to cause Me to change My mind where you will spend eternity is in error. For that day at The Judgment, the judgment will already be done; all that will be left is the sentence. There will be No chance of deliverance then, no chance of turning away from it then and no opportunity to make any choice then. No chance to repent or make anything right. You will have just run out of time and that may happen tomorrow. Because you are young that doesn't mean you won't face that day possibly real soon.

Revelation 22:10-12 'and he saith unto me, Seal up the sayings of the prophecy of this book: for the time is at hand. He that is unjust, let him be unjust still: and he who is filthy, let him be filthy still: and he that is righteous, let him be righteous still: and he that is holy, let him be holy still. And, behold, I come quickly; and my reward is with Me, to give every man according as his work shall be'. Whatever state you meet Me in, is the state of being you will remain throughout all eternity. The line gets drawn, no more chances. Repent today.

PART VII

POSSESS A GODLY ATTITUDE

> Thy servant slew both the lion and the bear: and this uncircumcised Philistine shall be as one of them, seeing he hath defied the armies of the Living God.
> (I Samuel 17:36)

WHILE IT IS true that you need to develop an attitude, you must desire the best attitude, because if that attitude is not to die for Me to live in you, then what can you accomplish for Me? The attitude of the vessel who is writing this book has always been that of 'If I die, I die, but I will not glorify the enemy and go down in believing that I have no power to overcome. If God doesn't save me, then if I perish, so I perish. But I will not relinquish my belief that God loves me and desires the best for me. If I'm poor, I'm poor but I will always believe that God desired more for me.'

I heard a very famous so-called prophetess tell her people that they had to have the attitude of a bulldog. This was painful for Me to watch because she was talking to a people that I called to peace and forgiveness. She was listening to the voices in that church that claimed that I would take from My people who worked hard to learn and was given wisdom by Me to earn wealth. A people that I had it planned to bless if they would give up their past hurts and forgive instead of fighting and coveting and taking. They were told about the transference of funds that I would take from those who earned it and give to those who did not. ALL of you were given the same measure of faith. ALL did not use it well. It is not the fault of the one who used it well that the one who was more like Cain. Your modern day Able was accepted by Me but those who believed the lies of Cain in their lack of forgiveness and hatred for Me they decided to covet and forget My word. Just toss it aside and go and take what they lied to themselves belonged to them. Had they been the people the great people I called who had grace and mercy in their hearts, where forgiveness should have reigned. Had they listened to my voice instead of these evil ones who lusted for more and did not care what happened to My people. They never would have developed in so much evil against My word. So they threw My Word out so they may obtain in greed what they accused their brother of. Color doesn't matter it was brother against brother because of envy, jealousy, hatred.

This vessel who wrote this book suffered and endured hardship and persecution that was unbelievable and yet never once did she not rejoice because those who claimed to be Mine were rich. Wake up people see where you have gone, see what you should have done and repent that I may heal your land in your heart. I will never take from one who earned it and gives to one who hasn't no matter what the reason. This vessel was poor for years and years. Coming out of the slums but she never raised a hand in her heart or mind against anyone or coveted their money or property. That is My Son Jesus Christ in her.

Every step, every thought that this vessel took was always giving Me all the glory. That attitude holds a lot of weight with Me. Without a heart that has been completely cleansed by the blood of Jesus, without a mind that has completely led every thought captive to Christ through the Word and the presence of the Holy Spirit; all through obedience to the Word and allowing Jesus Christ to take up an abiding residence in you; it is impossible to accomplish. You will always find yourself enduring temptation to the flesh when it can be overcome in the Word. Get the attitude that is willing to go through anything, endure anything to obey Me in the Word and by your faith in the Word I will honor you as I have honored her. All of My prophets must have this attitude, for this attitude leaves no place for the flesh, the world or the devil. 'Thy will be done, not Mine but Thine.' That is the attitude of Jesus Christ.

Don't you yet understand? When you promised or still promise anyone that God will take away what rightfully belongs to another you are teaching them covetousness? How can I be with you when you tell them that I will take away from others and give to them? That is insane when I said if you don't work you don't eat. If you say that you did not have a chance you are very wrong. Because I gave every soul the same measure of faith and it was all about how you chose to use it. You chose to use yours to learn how to steal they chose to work hard for it. You never should have listened to your leaders. I don't suggest anyone go up to any pastor and rebuke them because I did not call you to do that. I suggest if you know they are in error not to stay there to become partakers of their evil deeds. Just get up and walk away and don't look back. Don't lift them up in a prayer of any kind except to tell Me that you know I AM not with them because they go against Jesus by going against His word.

PART VIII

DIVIDED AGAINST YOURSELF?

And Jesus knew their thoughts and said unto them, every kingdom divided against itself is brought to desolation, and every city or house divided against itself shall not stand; (Matthew 12:25)

THE AMERICAN DREAM that everyone speaks about or thinks about is only obtainable by My grace. I cause it to rain on the just and unjust alike. Success never means that you are right, that you are pleasing to Me, nor does it mean that it is My will. But many of you apply those thoughts and principals to what you think is Me. It is because so many are very mistaken and in such a perilous condition of their soul, that I state these things clearly and precisely out of My great love for My people.

You have been taught in error what is important. While people sell you the gospel and tell you that God told them if you give them your money (even if it is your last penny) that God will take this scripture and bless you with it. Don't you know? Don't you understand that all the scriptures are blessing in the LORD belong to you? Don't you see how they rob you while they ask you for more money repeatedly? This vessel was told by Me not to ask you for one penny. And she doesn't. She promises you nothing not even a blessing if you listen to her. I have revealed to her that if she tells you what to do with your money that she is covering what you have earned. And if she dares tell you in My Name that I would bless you if you even follow her. Because she knows that she did not die for you; she knows that she did not comfort and keep you all these years. And she doesn't dare judge or condemn you if you give or don't give for she is not your judge.

She brings you a message and tells you that if I the LORD lay it upon your heart to give to her or to her ministry that is between you and the LORD.

She tells you that she doesn't want you trying to follow her. She knows if you try to become like her you will stumble and fall and fail. She knows that you need to strive to be like Jesus in your life with your personality. She knows that you need to follow Him according to your life the way He raised you, what and how He worked with you and let Him lead you into all truth and let Him lead you to repentance until the operation of your soul is finished. Not to have power over anyone, or be better or greater than anyone. Not to use it in unrighteousness but to do the works of the LORD. For many, many years she knew she had more than any teacher or preacher and yet she never touched it to show she had anything. She was under obedience to Me to be silent at all times and never speak unless I called her. Some would say to her "Why don't you go to so and so and ask him for his pulpit? You preach so much better than he does." She would say "I don't want his pulpit if I have a pulpit I want the one God gives me; I want my own. So nothing will make me ever take one step ahead of what God has for me in His time". She waited forty years and a week after she said that someone offered her own radio show.

From beginning to the end of this book, I have but one desire and that is to help anyone who wants to be able to see themselves the way I see them, that they may change their attitude towards Me, their feelings towards Me, and change their ways. Many of you are driven by your emotions; you are controlled by them. The thoughts of consequences concerning your decisions never come, and most of the time fear is your main driven factor. You desire to change, and as much as you desire a change for your life; as God so do I. For I love you. But I will always honor My Word. And you will not always like that. And when you are in opposition to it, then you are in opposition to yourself. For no choice ever hurts or disturbs Me and MY purpose. It can and will only destroy you, and because of that, I (the Lord) write this book. I have a continual unconditional love that strives to change your mind and your heart until the day that it is all too late; then there is no more time to change.

There are those who go out to other countries. But I must warn those from other countries I do not call anyone outside of this country to prophecy over anything in this country each prophet has his own territory in his own country so I call each one to his own place. Stay where you are called. You enter in and touch when you have no idea of what is really going on, and you make yourself look great to many, but I Am not well pleased. Someone from another country prophesied who the last President would be and how righteous he thought the man was. Had he known me he never would have taken something so tremendous in responsibility and say such a thing. He would have known how bad the man was for this country. But both of them being from two different places in the world did not belong here. No man from another country should ever be President of the United States and that makes the "birther" problem very important to this nation. Those who hide the truth will answer to Me.

This nation is divided against itself and has been for a long time. I Am speaking to the ones who claim to know Me through the Word and claim to have My Holy Spirit. Those of you who attend church also have done so much to cause this nation to be practically split right down the middle. All of you who call yourself by My name see it and know it. This isn't any great secret. The secret is that many of you have simply given up and quit believing the Word. This part of this book was written in 2007. But now it is different because the prophecy that I gave this vessel that she did not give in this book then is nowhere.

She saw two kinds of people in church worshipping Me. One was obedient and so blessed in the Spirit. The other played so many games with Me, My word, and My Holy Spirit. They did not want Me but it was not manifest yet how much they really hated Me. The disobedient suddenly saw how blessed the right was that they instantly became angry, jealous and filled with hatred. This the same old story of Cain and Able. So they raised their hand right in My sight to kill the obedient. This is exactly what they are trying to do right now. One group of individuals kicked Me out of their meetings and took on things that were not of Me. And many of you who don't know what is true or not because you never took it to Me. You just presumed. You became a partaker of their evil deeds. By voting for them, claiming once a certain party you will never change. The parties of years ago are not the same today. No such thing as a party for the people. They are out for self.

Right now I have to interject some truth to this hour. "Behold the man that God has called to restore this nation." Every President is anointed for this nation except for those who rejected right in My house the White House. But this 2018 President embraced My Anointing and I hold My word against you when you dare touch him. "touch not Mine anointed do them no harm." They have tried to harm him and his family from every direction you can find. To this day he strives to do what I have revealed to him that is right even to protect this nation from invaders disguised and take advantage of your generosity.

For years in this country, you have been led astray to take care of others first when you needed to clean this place up. Preach and teach the truth here and save the children who have ripped apart, raped and murdered daily while you play your games in church pretending you are Mine because you went to church. Your heart is far from me and he is very near to Me because he heard what you did not hear, nor did you want to hear it. When he warned you with the "snake" you refused to pay attention. Now it is at the border and I tell you that no matter what political party you belong to both of you will not be able to control what the left is striving to unleash. These people have no natural affection for their children that they can use them to obtain what is not theirs are in sync with those on the left who have no natural affection for anyone.

You have studied for years and still go into error. He isn't like you in a sense and the "fake news" no matter who they are that doesn't tell the truth would like you to look at the past that has been forgiven by the LORD Jesus Christ. What I have cleansed let no man call unclean. And if you don't believe that, you will see your life filled with your past evil never forgiven even at the judgment. At the time of your life that you face Me you will have to say that you forgive him for his past and you are sorry you gave him so much heartache and pain no matter who you are or how much money you have or what position you hold. I promise you that you will admit your sin or face eternity in your sin. Because you hindered a whole nation when you stopped him from doing his job because My Son's own words are that if you don't forgive you won't be forgiven. Many of you are applying the word wrongly. You apply compassion wrongly. This day above all days is more evil than you ever dreamed. If someone sins against you if you forgive them without demanding repentance then you give them a license to sin against you. You demand everything of this President but you demand nothing from the one who labored to destroy the country and you demand nothing from those who came to invade it. You call evil good and good evil. You reward evil and curse the good. You need a good dose of the fear of the LORD.

This is not the same as letting in people into this country as it was years ago. You must understand that you have to take care of your own first, your own country and your own country's children first. This is why he says America First. I revealed to him the truth that will set you free if you accept it.

There is an anointing on every President that comes into office. I the LORD in the presence of My Holy Spirit lead, guide and direct every leader of this nation except for the ones who rejected Me once they got into office. Except for the ones who told the people that they were Christians to get votes and once they got in there they were able to do the worse evils such as worshipping other gods; they seem to be able to work to destroy the Ten Commandments which guided our laws for decades. Or they did the worst sexual acts in the White House until it had to be cleaned out of every demon and devil in it. When you vote someone in office even if they deceive you and lie it is your responsibility to know that their own culture gives permission to lie to achieve finding out your weakness and using it against this nation to obtain access to it. And you are so foolish that you vote for any of them? Your vote has consequences when you didn't care if they got hurt by these people remember it can and will come upon you. Do not support evil such as abortion or persecution of Israel. Here are My two major important issues right now. Do not support open borders for the invasion of this country.

This man who is now in office got saved in office. He receives the LORD the way you ought to. But because he has not done it as long as you have all of you take advantage of him and think that I AM as blind as you are. The decisions he made from the very beginning proved his love for this nation in his limited knowledge of the Bible.

I used him to cause people all over the world to admit there is and was a day that My Son was born by acknowledging Merry Christmas. The whole world knows that it is the day that My Son was born. If you took a day; any day it could have been in your heart that day and I found no fault in you taking a day to honor My Son by giving gifts. These people who fuss about things of no meaning, such as trees decorations etc. My people don't know that and they use it now to honor My Son. How dare you to judge them for not doing it your way? You fuss over things that mean nothing because you want to be heard, seen and understood. I don't care. Those who call themselves My church leaders or prophets sit so high in judgment and fight over nothing and left out the weightier matters and that is why the sinners they detest so much will get in before them. Church leaders did not die for you why do you let them judge and condemn someone to not have My Son because you are not of their religion, or not of their doctrine etc. Did they die for you? Did they hold your hand and comfort you when you needed it and you needed to be healed? No common sense.

Yes, you should support a leader once I put him or her in office, but you should never speak for any man except to say that you believe that I called him or her for this hour in this nation, and after they take office, you then need to support them in prayer. But never support a president who believes it is alright to kill babies or worship other gods. These are atrocities If I speak for him that is a different story and I Am speaking for him because you demand perfection when you are not perfect.

You listen to evil gossip and lies hour after hour on the so-called news. Trashing your President is not news. It is evil and they twist and turn it. Those who pose for pictures as close to porn as you can get all those who are cleansed doing porn. Adulterers and adulteresses bring up people's past and destroy them with it while they have done worse. But if this nation falls to such a point that an ungodly person takes office that believes it is alright to kill the innocent and I am speaking of babies. That they can see their grandchildren destroyed because they view the baby as a punishment to their children who perhaps made a mistake. Do not support them in your prayers, for you are asking Me to be partaker of evil and I will not. You become a partaker of them and I will not support you. I am not speaking of their past I am speaking about them doing these things while they are in office. Which means they did not repent nor intended to.

Some of them are worshipped; singers who sound good and some of them are worshipped. Silly little girls think they are so sexy. Silly people are their following. Women past the age of thinking such silliness speak of some men being sexy. I Am not against anyone because they are of a certain race, ethnic background, or gender. What I Am against is when that person does things or says things and claim that I Am with them. Have you not read that you will be judged by your words and by those words you will either stand or fall? To the point that even now what you have said in the past comes out into the open because I put it forth into the light.

Every person who claims Jesus Christ has a certain amount of righteousness within Him even those with the most limited amount of knowledge of the Word. But not every man lives what he claims to believe. From the worldliest person to the godliest, those portions of the Word can be seen if they ever had anything to do with Jesus' Word. I wrote clearly in My Word that you will know them by their fruits it is not the number of people that they are not able to persuade. By their fruits, you shall know them. You must ask yourself; do the people that I am tempted to support think it is alright to destroy, kill, a helpless life within a woman's body? Do you honestly believe that I would take part in such a thing, to being as evil as a man or a woman who would willfully and deliberately destroy the helpless individual living within a woman? All that I created, all that I put into the intricate miracle of birth. How impossible it is for anyone to become pregnant except by a miracle, and I would give permission to willfully and deliberately kill it as though it was not made in My image. Because you still don't get it. I choose who is born, and who is not. The Supreme Court doesn't do it, parents don't do it, doctors don't do it. I AM the only One who has the right to decide who lives and who dies. No one else is qualified to make a decision about someone that I created.

Read Romans what happens when you take the image of the Creator and turn it into the image of the creature which is a man. When you tell a woman she has a right to choose to destroy her child. Right there you changed My image to be like yours. You then made yourself God. Those of you who support the left because you think you saw what our President used to do or was accused of doing and forget the power of the blood of Jesus to cleanse every soul who asks for it. Forget that right before your eyes this man is learning about God and the things of God and you are helping others play with him and destroy him all because you think that I AM with you in it.

Listen to what I AM about to say here. A person is called but they are still free moral agents able to make decisions that can put a halt on that call. Therefore until it is fulfilled with their permission so to speak they are not in the fulfillment of it. I will tell you exactly the day I the LORD decided that he would be President. It was at a debate when he talked about abortion. He wasn't acting; he talked about the unborn with a passion only My children have. You can go back and see it clearly that is the moment that he won My heart was when he spoke from the heart his reasons for being against abortion. I marveled at it how so many of you read My word, claimed My word, sat before the preaching of My word and still you are as blind as a bat. He by nature had more than you had after years and years of reading and studying and attending church.

Why, because he wasn't sick and I came to save those who needed to be made whole. He had and has a healthy mind which focuses on what is right and Jesus is the King of Righteousness, therefore, he follows the LORD while he is in the White House. Is he perfect? No, no man, no woman is perfect and the only perfect One was Jesus Christ. And you need to leave this President alone even in prayer except to ask for wisdom, power, knowledge understanding to defeat the enemy of your soul and this nation. Pray that he gets the respect and honor due to his office because he is one of a few that have not defiled it.

My church needs to be wise in their decisions of choices in life. I have said clearly in Roman chapter 13. That when you do right you will have praise from authority and if you don't then you need to be afraid. If you have done anything that you should not have done and think you can just sweep it under the rug without repentance you are wrong. I respond to honesty. Not the person who says they know the people want them to be honest, but they in their doings are not. But all of you live your lives as though I don't exist. And the shock of it all is you claim the highest in the churches. This is why so many left the church. They did not ever leave Me they left churches that did all the things written in this book.

This nation is polarized by two extremes. You can see the extremes in the world clearly, but do you have enough wisdom to see them spiritually? On the one side, there are those who have the Word, or at least some knowledge of it. They want no parts of the Holy Spirit; they deny that God does anything today, that all of it was in the past, that God today is dead, no longer powerful enough to do what He used to do through His children. They do things their way all the while they claim Me. Some are so sure that God doesn't want them asking for help even though they read that they were to become like little children which depend upon their father. On the other side, you have those who claim the Holy Spirit is in operation today as He was then, yet they never get into the Word because they love Me, they only get into it to obtain their needs or wants. Because both are disobedient; Try to bring the two together and it is like the pull of two equally powerful magnets face to face, they will repel one another. When they are in opposition they repel, but if they got on board and got together and worked alongside then they would not repel one another. One side would have to accept the Holy Spirit as written in the book of Acts and the other would have to get completely into the Word. Now I Am not speaking of a people who just because they seem to follow the word and they seem to be unspotted from the world are to be joined with for many are worse hypocrites. I Am speaking of those who through experience with the LORD Jesus Christ allowed Him to live and reign in their hearts and minds so that He could write His laws upon the tables of their hearts.

By your own lives and actions, you prove to Me daily that you want no parts of My Word. And they want no part of My Spirit. And there are those who really want no parts of the truth in Christ to reign in them they only repeat the word and play with it and use it to their purpose. Oh, I know, you say that's not so. Ask yourself how many times do you pick up the Word and read it let alone ponder it and meditate on it. Ask yourself how many times you did this just to know Me and understand Me. Not how many times you picked it up to save yourself from circumstances, situations, afflictions, financial crisis etc. How many times do you pick it up just to get to know My Son that died for you? Both sides claim Me, both sides reject Me. You don't think so. Read on and you will see.

On the other side, you have all the traditions that you think you are following according to Me. You have a form or a formula you operate in. You made the decision that I Am not the same today as I was yesterday and because of that, you became entangled in things of no importance, things that don't mean anything. So you continued in your refusal to believe that the Holy Spirit is given to you giving you the power to seek Me in My Word that I may lead you into the truth. The book of Acts was written for all to realize that what I did then, I do now, how I worked with people I work now. But no, you chose to deny Me, therefore, you deny your self the benefits of everything that I left for you. And why are you so deluded because you received not the love of the truth?

Your brother is not someone who believes in another god. It is not someone who worship's Satan. It is not someone who does evil such as written in the Word. Your brother or sister is someone who belongs to Jesus Christ not because they say so but because I witness that they are Mine by their fruits. So that doesn't mean to accept those who say they have the word and live like demons. I Am not telling you to accept a person because they are a certain color, nor do not accept them because they are not a certain color; what I Am telling you is that color has nothing to do with it. All of you are brothers if you belong to Me. And if you belong to Me you will know them by their fruits. And the fruits of Mine do not include destroying the innocent who are helpless to defend themselves. Nor do they include blessing same-sex marriages.

Being cruel to these people is not of Me. You do not live within the realm of My will so what are you doing judging them? Being gracious, kind and condoning are two different things. Why do you dare to judge someone you know nothing about because you know nothing about Me.

There is a line to be drawn. A line that says I will be there if you need me. All of these things are something done against themselves. I do not lift a finger against them; they are against themselves when they disobey My Word. They have a right to visit each other in the hospitals, they have a right to choose a lot of things, but they have no right to expect the same blessings of a union between a man and a woman. But you have no right to go and tell them that. How they live is none of your business. If they ask your advice or seek your truth then you have a right to speak. But to force what you believe on people is not of Me. When they make their commitments without Me, then they must realize they will suffer the consequences of their choices. It is not your job to even hate their sins, it is not your job to destroy them, or hurt them or even deny them, Christian love. I have witnessed famous Senators, preachers, Congressmen at a service where the preacher holds up My Word and screams to kill the homosexual because it says in the word that they are to die. Not so I did not say that. I did not say that you were to kill anybody. All of you are worthy of death in the sins that you commit but Jesus died so that you did not have to. It is your Christian responsibility to be there when they have important needs for prayer in the hopes that they will see that I love them and repent. It is up to you to help them realize the error of their ways without enticing hatred. There are those who went into other countries and preached without realizing the consequence of preaching the word with hatred. Caused the leader of that country to drown these people and put into prison anyone who talked to them. Some preachers go so far as to go into detail behind the pulpit to describe what these people do in their private homes.

Even as I say this I AM not telling you that the treatment of always being there to help someone who constantly spits in your face and works to hurt and destroy Me in your nation. Because I did say turn the other cheek but I meant in the brethren. You were to take the wrong among the brethren. To not fight, not sue, not destroy etc. But you are not to allow the soulless come into your home through invasion and kill your children and think that it was and is My will. I assure you that it is not My will. I would not have told the disciples to sell all that you have and go and buy a sword if I did not intend for them to defend themselves against people who are soulless. You can call some animals if you like but animals act better. I don't see any animals raping and plundering and killing just for the fun of it and bathing in the blood. They do what they do for food.

The truth is I didn't tell one person anywhere in my word to kill these people. I did not tell one person in the word that I hate them. I hate what they do but listen to this I hate what you do also. I am speaking of homosexuality now. I led no one to stand at funerals and say that I hate them. I hate no one. I hate what people do but not and never them. I Am NOT with the preachers who pick up the Bible swing it over their heads and scream God says kill them. They lie on Me and say the Word said it not me. He (meaning Me as the One he is talking about) says they should be killed. No so. This kind of preacher lies on Me and if you go to his meetings and humble yourselves and bow your head in respect because you think he has Me I assure you that you may die the death that he is calling for on others. Because never in my word did I say they are to be put to death. I said they are worthy of death. But so are you who do the same kind of things; those of you who do evil. I did say that you know they are worthy of it but I also said that you judge them and you will not escape judgment for doing so. Read Romans chapter 1 and chapter 2. My intention is that all men be saved and as long as there is breath; there is a chance for life. Many have been saved without anyone destroying them. You did not die for them why in the world would I permit you to kill anyone when you are worthy of the same thing for different reasons?

Now if I chose to bless you here, or in heaven that is something that you are entitled to in Christ, but never to hurt another to get it. Remember Jezebel and Ahab, they took what they thought belonged to them also. She whispered a lie into his ear. Since he was a king all he had to do was murder the real owner and take it. Have you not heard that it is wrong to covet what another has and claim that because you don't have it that I would rob someone to give it to you? What is the matter with you? Because you are without gives you no right to demand to have what belongs to another, what they labored for. If they applied themselves to educate themselves enough to earn something, why would I just give it to you? These are things that split this nation. Don't you see that if a person is qualified and earned the right to have certain jobs I gave no permission to take from them and give to those who are not qualified?

A house divided cannot stand. If you are not loyal to your own country, how can you ever be loyal to Me? If you are not loyal to your own family, how can you be loyal to Me? Those babies that are being destroyed are your children, your family and in some case your grandchildren. How can you desire to destroy these by believing that it is a punishment to make a woman go through the pregnancy because you view a member of your family a punishment, therefore, they must be destroyed. Where I ask you is your mind; what in the world are you thinking? Listen, those of you who preach that I will give and give and give because you feel sorry for people who are struggling, because of their need. You need to examine why you go against My Word. Because a person is in need and many times it is because they do not properly manage what they have, they don't even desire to find out how to change and you tell them that they have something coming from Me if they believe My Word; you need to read again, I taught no such thing. When you give to someone who did not earn it they have no appreciation for it and it troubles them inside that you gave, so slowly they begin to hate you. Hate you because they needed you and hate you because every time they see you they are reminded they owe you. Make no mistake they will not appreciate you or love you for giving to them.

Justice is justice, right is right, doing things the right way, and obtaining things the right way; with hard work, determination, developing the abilities and gifts that I gave you would bring prosperity to you. But it doesn't fall from heaven if you are not qualified. You say you are qualified by faith. Where have you ever gotten the impression that simply because you believe something it is My will or My way? You may have seemed a power to operate and obtain, but I assure you it is not from Me. Some are so foolish that just because they need or just because they cried and cried before Me that I will answer and hear when they are depending on My mercy while they never give any mercy to anyone; they will wait and wait in vain.

It is time up ahead and very soon to separate. Time is coming to release the angels to separate those who are Mine and those who are not. Oh, that's right. There is no such thing as the 'rapture'. No one is going to be left behind. All of you are Christians and all of you are going up. You know the Word which is Jesus, that's all just symbolism, it's just a story doesn't mean a thing. Just keep on doing what you are doing; just keep on splitting your nation right in half. Right down the middle. There are more so-called reborn Christians in this nation than the few that shows up when the time comes to vote. This was written before the Silent Majority decided to come out and vote and when they did they voted Trump in. Read Malachi 3 how that when you throw your hands up in the air and say it is no use to continue to serve the LORD; you literally give the wicked the power to do whatever they want. They have no interest in what happens to their nation and they take interest only just before the time. Then they expect Me to tell them who to vote for. They don't do their homework of reading My Word that they may have discernment enough to recognize who is who, so they trust in the media to give them the truth and as it is right now, they lie. Discernment comes from knowing the Word of God.

This was written long before Fake News was recognized. The News organizations for years told the people who to vote for. And they were respected and followed and played God for our nation. No one ever realized what they were doing until the Silent Majority woke up. They are of the world and they will paint it all to make it look like they want. This was written in 2007 and I revealed from the get-go what was happening in the nation to this vessel. She could feel the power of both parties voting. She could feel the fight for control of the nation. Both seemed almost equal but because of the Silent Majority not voting I (the LORD) took it as they must want this man in office if they didn't they would have voted. So she felt Me release the power to get this person in as President and she heard Me say "I will give them exactly what they asked for". By not voting they were asking for what happened for the next eight years. The United States began to become the most lawless nation in order to usher it into globalism. In order to bring in another culture to control this great nation that I (the LORD) created to be Christian. Look at the Ten Commandments as an example of what was in all your laws. This vessel grew up in a time that it was in the air not to lie, not to steal, not to cheat. You knew it and no one had to teach it; you felt the power of the law in the air. A few didn't obey and were considered lawless. But most of the nation was Christian. Reading the Bible every day before classes started. You all had prayer and pledged allegiance to the flag of the United States of America. As surely as I chose Israel to be a peculiar people, so did I choose this nation to have Jesus Christ as the peculiar people. They are parallel. Bless a Jew and I bless you. Curse a Jew and I curse you. Bless a Christian and I bless you, curse a Christian and you curse yourself.

And you who claim to be Mine listen to them even when I reveal a clear difference, you permit them to use their words and ways to convince you that you need someone the world loves. You by reading filthy rags that call themselves news destroy My people help destroy one who will live for Me and stand up for My principals. You always forget that everyone is human and makes mistakes. But those who never turn from those mistakes are the ones you need to watch out for.

If a person when they are young poses for pictures that in their culture they don't see as wrong. Then comes here and belongs to Me enough to not do that anymore then she has been cleansed by the blood of Jesus Christ. But when a porn star demands respect without ever admitting that what she is doing is wrong and worse yet is proud of being what she is and she wants respect and you are ignorant enough to think that I would bless such a woman. You are wrong. You have no godly wisdom to discern Who I Am. When a man is young before he becomes President and he does things and repents of them and goes into the White House cleansed by the blood that is one thing. But when he believes there is no god who sees, hears and knows what he is doing and does one of the worst acts in history with a woman then he hasn't changed, he is not cleansed by the blood of Jesus because there is no repentance of sin. Wake up and understand many continue in the evil they have been doing for years and years and yet you let the media lift them up and don't vote against them. "Sigh". I weary of you.

When a man comes into the office and knows nothing compared to many Bible scalars follows simple principals of the Bible than by his own nature as written in the word he is following Me and Me alone. Yet many of you who sit so high dare to call him unclean and dare to remember his past as though you have none. You put yourself in a position of being judged for what you won't forgive those who repented of it. These people have become so foolish. Can you escape judgment? It says so in My Word. No! Play as you might you will never escape the LORD who gave His life that you might live if you only confess and make it right. The left ignores the wrongs of these people who don't repent and you listen. I forgive and forget those who strive to do right now and you listen to evil.

And there are those who use their churches to feed hatred, discord, etc. Fight and devour and what will be your reward even if you seem to win. For what good will it does to gain the whole world and in the end lose your own soul. Continue to hate and be resentful, the only purpose that I intended for you to take a firm stand upon was My Word. Never did I intend for you to fight for a man or a woman to become something that they are not. Well, you're loyal in one place and that is to your gladiators, your sports heroes, your movie stars. Very loyal to your rock stars and anyone else that you worship in My place. I have nothing against these things, what I hate is you putting them in My place. You take their words and opinions above Mine. The saddest part of all of this is how many of you claim to belong to My Son. The saddest thing is when you don't know, and it is all because you have not made it your business to know My Son's Word. And worse yet when you do get into it which is seldom you then judge according to the eyes not righteously.

I know that some of you are suffering and have been suffering and it has been for generations. I know that you believe that I will deliver you from the people that you think are responsible for hurting you and your family for generations. Those generations were the first that you were to forgive and not carry it, teaching hatred to your children and your children's children, using it all for an excuse for permitting your lives to be wasted and to steal from others out of bitterness of heart and evil intentions. And I know that you praise Me, and you wait on Me, and you expect that because you are poor and needy that I will not forsake you, and that I will lift My hand to deal with whom you believe is responsible. And when you think someone is against you, that they will fall into their own self-made pits. And in some cases, you actually believe that these people are going to hell. And since I don't move against them then you begin to pray for their death or work to get it done somehow, someway. You ask Me for justice and judgment upon those whom you are convinced in your heart that they are responsible. You want these people to put in fear; you want them to be held accountable. All as though you are perfect because you do praise Me, and you do witness on occasion, and tell of My marvelous works. You also believe and give Me the glory by the fact that you know that had it not been for Me, you would have been dead long ago. All of these things are not enough to cause Me to bring judgment on any soul that you think has done you evil. I will never send a soul to hell because of your contrived offense.

You take My Word and apply it according to what you think destroyed your ancestors, destroyed all your chances of ever coming out of what has been done in the past and none of what you believe according to your thinking is true. Not that those you are against are innocent. But it is not up to you to make these judgments. And your leaders feed you this because they are in error. Some of you are innocent of this, but most are waiting for me to judge someone else. You don't realize the seriousness of the state that your soul is in. If and when I come to judge, I will judge you first. Judge not lest ye be judged for what judgment you meet will be met unto you. Want to hold someone accountable, and you can't wait until they pay? You will be the first held accountable and the first to pay to make no mistake my word is true. I promise you that you will suffer to the uttermost that dare goes up to any of My children and say "I'm taking what you have." You are a thief and a liar and an abuser of men. And I want it clearly known you have no part in Me.

Without ever obeying My Word by getting into it to know My Son, you have left the door open to bring judgment upon yourself with this attitude. I know, you're taught to take what is yours. But you have taken it upon yourself to believe what you believe and you are striving to take what belongs to others. And believing anything will never make it so, especially when it comes to these things. I did not lead you there in your thinking. Bitterness, resentment, envy, jealousy, greed and many more things including your church leaders led you into that belief. And when that bitterness rose up in any one of you, then many were defiled even to whole churches. You then become guilty of what you hate and claim that I desire to deliver you of. And I do indeed desire to deliver you. True deliverance is never by the problem going away. It is always obtained in victory by you retaining the truth of the Word within you no matter what your circumstances, or condition. The truth that needs to be retained is that you do not curse those that you think destroyed your life. You are responsible for your life, not anyone else. You are responsible for your choices, not anyone else.

True deliverance is by being able to have the fruits of the Holy Spirit within you and that cannot come about as long as you do n't forgive one person or one offense. You are to forgive every ancestor, yours and theirs. Both are guilty because all are human. No matter how you paint it, no one is ever completely right on either side. The only One who is completely right is Jesus. As long as you hold on to the anger, resentment, and bitterness, you are not retaining the knowledge of Me which is manifested by the fruits that you bear. If your fruits are not unconditional love, then you do n't have all the rest of them. You oppose yourselves and hinder your own soul, and blame everyone else for the problem. And you need to repent. I can't help you in this condition of life; My hands are tied by you. Just think this is happening today on a big scale. Many people are in this condition because they listened to the lies of their church leaders and in the nation, they listen to the lies of media withholding the truth. When a few years back a so-called pastor said God damn America and he did exactly what many of you did in secret. You cursed your country by promising other countries they would have your country. I AM not with you. You cursed your own country when you had leaders that kept saying America will pay instead of praying for My mercy to be upon her and lead her to repentance. My church leaders were not to be her judge. They were not to be the judge of a nation that they live in.

I look and look and look and with all of these things going on in the church and the nation it is very hard to move when none deserve Me to move. I listened to My children cry out and turn from their wicked ways not stay in them and be proud of the evil they seem to accomplish.

If you want things within your gender, or your ethnic groups then do things according to My Word and do them righteously, not with evil motivations that have such self-interests that you can think of yourself as some sort of savior. Many of you talk a lot about this nation need to think of others and not themselves. But all you have on your mind is achieving what your agenda is. All you see is what you suffer and how badly you want to be delivered and being a Christian is so much more than that. Save your own nation's children before you reach out to save those who don't care about their own children. Those children are the responsibility of their own countries and their own parents. You can't pick up any child or any mother and claim I led you to deliver them when I led you to deliver your own in this nation first.

You have gone so far that you believe that anybody that disagrees with you hates you or hates your gender or your group. And the media knows that you don't really believe that but they feed you with that until your so ignorant you believe them and act as they say. Wow, how much control you give the enemy through the media to destroy you and your nation and Christianity. Anybody who doesn't do what you think in your minds is your enemy, not Mine, but yours and you take it as though they hate you, or your gender, or your ethnic group. The way I Am describing it is the way it is in you. You believe you are humble because you are in need and you cry to Me and you turn My Word to work for you to apply it where and when you want it without ever truly seeking Me to apply it to you enough to be kind, gently forgiving, meek, long-suffering, peace, great peace to those who have it. The humble heart My Word speaks of is humble and contrite which is sorry for their sin. Not always crying because they are in need and most of the time they are in need due to their inability to overcome their own weaknesses which is first selfishness. Or they are lusting for something and have no godly contentment and will never be satisfied.

There are those of you who don't understand the word humility. Because you get on your knees and cry to Me because you need because you hurt; that doesn't make you humble. If you were humbled, you would not dare come to Me as though I will destroy someone that you think is responsible for your condition of life. Many of you refuse to do the right thing with the life I gave you, and you refuse to find out how to do the right thing. Do you honestly believe that you have the power to persuade Me to send a soul to hell because you believe they are going there? All because they were not where you thought they ought to be or because they didn't do according to what you think. You think that they should do according to the things that are important to you.

Am I supposed to work according to this all because of your condition, your circumstances? If you let all of life, and all of your finances slip through your fingers and then expect others to hand what they worked for to you, where Am I in this? I am not like you. You do n't have control over Me. Oh, I see, you believe that I Am God and that I Am a rewarder of those who seek after Me diligently. And so I Am! And that somehow makes everything slanted on your side? You seek Me diligently for your need. Tell Me how is selfish, greedily taking My Word to your purpose is seeking Me diligently? You take part in the Word and use it to work for you. It is backward. You are supposed to work for Me. The Word is given for you to work for Me. Pick up your cross and deny yourself. How does that operate in your thinking? This is why I hold the church leadership so responsible. While they should have been teaching your principles of humility, obedience, dying to self-being willing to obey My will no matter what you think they taught you to name it and claim it. It is yours. All that My Son has in heaven is now yours take it. Don't you and they see that when you take it you are taking what doesn't belong to you and you wind up coveting?

The self-seeking media to make their living by running with any story, they reveal secrets that I never intended to be made known. They are irresponsible, and they take what these celebrities say as though it is Me. They take a leader of a great nation and they to expose what they think they have been able to make look like the truth and most of you swallow it. They really destroying of this nation they left alone. This is horrible.

If they choose to they hide what others do, and expose only what they want to persuade you in their corner of thinking and if you were praying for your leaders as I instructed you in My Word, you never would have helped them destroy this President, and you would have seen it and prayed for it. Many leaders of the past did much worse and none of it was ever exposed. Leaders are human beings, and all humans are flawed. Knowing this, My great love constantly strives to lead them to repentance. Yes, you have choices, on one hand, you see your life as you know it financially slipping away from you and you will choose someone you think who will be your savior where your money is concerned. Live deliciously, live with ease able to go anywhere, or do anything, at any time as I have always blessed you is one of your choices, the other is to destroy the innocent. Tell me how is that choice picking up your cross and denying yourself? At the end which choice do you think I will be pleased with?

I will not defend him because he is right; I will not defend him because he is perfect, nor because he hasn't made any mistakes. He claims My name and has made as many mistakes as those of you who are calling to destroy him have made. Why do any of you think that I don't destroy completely some of your former leaders? Was it because many of them were perfect? Was it because any man is worthy of being worshipped? It is because just as you would be in a marriage and in order for you to have the way you have to destroy the spouse. In that small realm of marriage, you then sever your right arm off. And you bleed for a long, long time. Both are guilty in the marriage because being one, you are not fully to blame on either side. So it is in this nation with its leaders, never is the full blame on them. As I said if you did not vote those you know are doing great evil to hold back the only one who isn't I would have more hopes for you. But you deliberately voted to stop him. It isn't the nation of the past where one balances the other. One desires to have a sovereign nation and the other desires to get his rule and reign over the whole world so he destroys the sovereignty.

Every person who is right now fighting to gain control has an agenda. You have witnessed them fight like Hitler did to obtain being incarnated by Satan. You on the left are watching those who fought among themselves knowingly fighting for the antichrist seat. You think they don't know whoever controls the USA will control the world? That is why I called one person that would stand up against globalism and you who do not support him even in midterms are responsible before Me for hastening the antichrist into being. Your President stands against these things. He doesn't fight for control of the world. He wants to help his own nation that is why he says America first. Understand the difference.

Your support in prayer, your blessings in speech and not curses for your President would have turned all of this around. You all will answer to Me for not holding up your leader in prayer. Yes, I love justice. But I hate it when those who are unjust call for it. I hate it when those who are not without sin expect Me to deliver someone into their hands. Those who deliberately go against My Word and make a mockery of what it says in My children; I do not support such people. But when one is faithful enough to stand up and say they believe in the sanctity of a marriage between a man and a woman, when they believe and confess it to the world that they are against killing innocent babies. I will stand up and protect them.

But when a man or a woman, fight to give anyone the right to kill an innocent human being, or fight to give marriage rights to those of the same sex, or take little children and torture them by touching their sex so they can have free course for their sin and free course to rape them. I most definitely with not defend them, nor will I stand up for them, for they have forsaken My word. And I will never go against My Word because My Word is Jesus Christ. Therefore when you choose them over Me, well ask yourself will I be with you when you need Me? Only for a season will Satan seem to give you comfort and take care of you because he knows your end. So if you seem to succeed remember My Word is true, and I have no darkness in Me at all.

If I dealt with you as harshly as you would have dealt with those who needed you to help them, to support them and you deserted them, there would be nothing left of you.

If life, the elements, and every force that Satan can send against you became the judgment that you so desire on this President, then I tell you right now, there would be nothing left of you. Judgment is easy to dish out. Why do you think I speak out against gainsaying, scorners, fault finders and such like? Because I hate all those evil works. I hate the works of the flesh that claim to have Me on their side. You never walked in the shoes of the man that you lie on and condemn. You have no idea what it is like. You strive and fight to obtain, and when you do, there is every evil work just as it says in My Word in the book of James. I show mercy to those who show mercy. You say he has no mercy? I say when did I die and make you God enough to judge what is in a man's heart. You have a right to see the fruits, but you have no right to destroy.

You leave criminals to go free, but you destroy many good men that I have sent to lead in the past. You don't care that a criminal mind has murdered, you just care that they do not have to pay so it is alright if they deny, deny, deny and never admit they did anything. You pray and pray and pray that a murderer go free because you have pity on him, he belongs to your group. Your counselors tell them as Christians to never admit their wrongs to anyone. And you believe that I Am with you to cover all the evil up and restitution or at least godly sorrow is never expressed. You think and feel justified as though I justified you. You forget justification can only come with a humble and contrite heart admitting their sin never denying it. And you're still doing that today.

You need to hope I do not treat him the way you think that I should because if I would need to, I would visit you first. And to all of you, he who is without sin cast the first stone. These things are so true to the hour of this day in this nation that I had to leave much of this in. Whatever Presidents before Trump suffered none of them ever went through the hell so many people have had against him all because they could not see he was the only one that I called to bring this nation to repentance of the evil that is done in secret and bragged about in the open. If you took on one little section of what he has to go through daily because people like you call yourself Christian and think you have the right to decide and judge without living what you preach. I tell you now repent or I will come and deal with each one personally. Beginning with the leaders in the My house that taught people in error. Make no mistake here I AM making and clear distinction here between those who once led this nation, and one who right now strives to do what is right with it. He is hated by these other leaders because his very existence proves how wrong they were. And the hypocrites killed Jesus My Son for the very same thing. As long as He was alive he was a reminder that they were not of Me. And that is how President Trump appears to many of you. His existence proves how wrong you are and your need for repentance. No, he is not the Christ but he is someone that I sent for this hour upon the church and upon the nation.

Do you rejoice when you think you caught someone at something? Do you rejoice when you are able to destroy someone and make them look as dirty as your mind? Do you get excited at the fact that you are able to make your money by destroying someone? And do you claim that I am with you because if you do, remember I take up no cause to destroy anyone in this nation on your ability to destroy? You are on your own. I said this here because I watched a woman rejoice that she destroyed this President and she still rejoices when she thinks she has found some contrived lie to destroy him. I tell her and you touch not Mine anointed do them no harm. I say the same to the man who used the Bible to go against the Bible just to destroy this President Donald Trump. Both of liars appear on the evil media one after another.

I will not prophecy to you who is going to win any election because I refuse to foretell the future. What happens to this nation depends on your choice. You will have no one to blame once you put who you desire in office. A prophet's job is much, much more than telling the future. Even though a prophet can and does do that. Some of you have the mind of those who run from place to place looking for someone to tell a future for you. What difference is there between you and a person who seeks a fortune teller? I sent prophecy to warn you of what is up ahead for you if you do not repent.

This is why My Jesus was hated because He told the truth and this is why My prophets were hated in the past because they told the truth, and they warned people to repent. They were not used to comfort those who were sinning. A prophet that comforts more than he can be used to warn is no profit to Me and the cause of Christ. When you give comforting prophecies for all remember that not all who claim to be Mine are Mine. One of the most important things for prophecy; is to warn. If I couldn't speak to you through prophecy then how can you see you're wrong and repent? Especially in this hour where so many have turned off the Word. Jesus told what was to come for this world. That was not His whole ministry. He rebuked and exhorted all through the New Testament. First when He walked on the earth and then through those that are His. You need to hear His voice in this hour upon the earth right now, His voice through those who are His can still be heard if you listen. The job of the Holy Spirit is to lead you to Christ. His job is to CONVINCE you of your sins. When you shut Him down you have trouble with Me and you will face the judgment sooner than you thought. You think because you are young you won't face anything think again.

How dare you touch judgment where the leader of your nation is concerned. You think he did wrong? Tell it to Me and you know what I will tell you, exactly what you are doing wrong. Why? Because where he is, what he is doing, what he does is none of your business. It is My business. I have the power to cause what belongs to me to stand or fall. When I speak about a President make no mistake I AM speaking about President Donald Trump. You didn't call him I did. He is hidden under the shadow of My wing. Do you have any idea of what that means? He set his love upon Me; therefore I have done with him what you can clearly see had you had your heart open to the truth. And if you don't have it open to the truth you need to pray that I open it. Millions of you will pray and have prayed against him, striving to destroy him and you will not be able to. Just as surely as millions of people in the ministry will pray to destroy this woman who dares to tell you the truth through Me.

In her radio message, she told all of you to gather by the millions and pray against her and it will do you no good because you have killed many of the LORD'S prophets but this one God will not allow you to destroy. She is the voice for the hour; she is My voice for NOW. I speak plainly through her so that no one can say they don't understand the language or say they couldn't grasp it. No one will have an excuse. Many believe in their doctrines, their traditions which have destroyed more souls than they claim to save. Many use my people as slaves while they sit rich as kings. Claiming that I gave it all to them as they steal by promising the gospel to be fulfilled only if you give them money.

The gospel is fulfilled and blesses you as you fulfill your promise to Me that you will pick up your cross and follow me daily and deny yourself. You pick out church goings, doing things in church but you don't pick out the things that mean so much more to Me; the weightier matters of life and death hanging in the balance for My people. You have lied to them the blessings belong to them. Just as surely as the wicked politicians lied to the people and took their money and made paupers out of them so did you. Hate her as you will and it will do you no good. Let me tell you something right here.

I saw and heard when you prayed against her. I saw and heard as you gathered in your counsels claiming to be apostles and knew she was praying at the altar and to keep your so-called king you tried to kill her as you stabbed her at the altar. (I am speaking of a spiritual experience of your counsel gatherings as apostles. Not asking her guilt or innocence but taking the word of liars.) I was there and watched everyone who lied on her to obtain whatever they were looking for while she strove for one thing only obedience to Me. Here I Am in her defense for you to see plainly that you were wrong and repent. As pastors, you think that I Am with you against her telling the truth that I called her to tell to give ALL of you an opportunity to repent. If it is not said you can still hide your evil and die in your sins and because I love you I chose her and I will save her out of your hands and have saved her. You can't pray against Me in her and see her fall. She will stand even if you think no woman has a right to speak like this. Because you didn't call her, you didn't die for her, you didn't heal her, you didn't comfort her, you didn't do one thing of value with her. You denied her all of her life and here I Am in her defense. And if you use this book to imitate her or say that I spoke thru you the way I speak through her I will not go easy I promise you for this message is so important for the whole church to understand so that they may be ready to meet Me and see Me as I Am not a man filled with tradition, doctrines made Me seem. But I AM GOD.

When you decided she was so powerful that you could not talk to her; you didn't realize that her power came from Me. When you decided that she had all the answers you forgot the only way that could be is if she had Me. When you plotted against her a listened daily to a novice scream and tell you that she was doing things that she never did or touched; he was screaming against Me. She was not aware of what evil you plotted I hid it from her so that at the Judgment you could not accuse her of one thing. She laid her head down and slept and thought about how to be good to you; how to help you and you stabbed her right in the back claiming I was with you. And I am here to tell you today I was not and I AM not with you or the likes of you.

Your job is to pull down Satan and his works. And you can't do that because you walk with Him. Never was it ever to pull down people. Your job is to bind Satan when you see his works. Never is it, or was it ever to touch the hair on the head of anyone who believes in Me. It is better for a millstone to be tied around the neck of the person who hurts one of these little ones who believe in Me. I call them all My children. And since you don't sit in My seat, and you don't see what I see, and you are disobedient, who are you? You're not the person that I called. You saw she was holy so you tried in your evil wicked minds to make her as evil as you are. You talked and talked and talked until you thought you made it and still she stands before me blameless and holy. But you don't.

Don't you know why people do n't hold anyone responsible for the things they did in political parties? It is because those who were supposed to do something to stop it were doing the same things. It came out today. When you are filled with sin you can't talk about conviction you can only pretend and play and bluster and lie but you can't pull Satan down because you walk with him. She can and does but you only pretend you do. This President can clean and drain the swamp because he is not filled with the evil that many of the politicians operate in.

Those of you who are self-righteous, those who pay too much attention to what you hear without ever being there have no clue as to what is really going on. You go by what you hear, and I told you to judge righteous judgment, not according to what you hear or even see. I never condemned you for the loss of My Son for you. Never did I get angry with you because you had sinned so much. He was without any sin and I gave Him up freely that you may be free and now you are demanding that someone else not be free? Where do you think this will take you? I never rose up and fought in a rage of anger and hatred against any of you. Never did I speak out and tell everyone all the things that you did in secret when you asked Me to forgive you. My Son covered it with His blood. I promise you now, that every one of you who is determined to bring harm or see to it that someone pays for what you think they did or are doing; I promise you that what you do and have done will be exposed. What people hear in the ear will be shouted upon the housetops about you. Just about the hour that you think you have everything all showed up to remember I Am God. Remember these words in black and white were written in 2007 before all this evil hit the earth through lawlessness in a nation that denied Me when I brought this nation to Myself and I will bring it back through President Donald Trump. And woe unto you who call yourselves by My Name Christian and you do not support him.

In your pride, self-righteousness, foolishness, and silliness are delivering up this nation to your enemies. As God, I have the right to be outraged and angry for you being forgiven while My Son paid, and I never was nor will I be outraged. And now you are being guilty, desire another to pay. Are you so much without wisdom that you can't see? The young men and women who gave their lives and their bodies will suffer more with your erasing the reason that they gave their lives. Don't you understand you erase their sacrifice and force them to feel as though what they did was in vain when I called them to the purpose of protecting you? You erase My Son's life through disobedience by not putting His Word into your heart and mind, or by applying the negative of the Word to everyone but yourself. If there is one soldier, man or woman who gave their life or their body to answer the call of this nation and you do these things that dishonor them, then it is on you. Even if you lost a child in any war for this country, you are dishonoring their loss and it is on you. I AM not speaking of heroes your sense of understanding no matter where they come from and claim but I am speaking of every truth Patriotic American that recognizes and loves this nation. Not one that uses the Constitution to claim anything. They don't use it to prove anything the defended it well.

Who are these people who enjoy the freedom of this country, the protection of it and speak evil of it? Why would you watch them at all? Why do you want them into this country? Why do you give them a voice by watching what they think, what they feel? All their excuses and reasons to justify themselves because they are afraid that they must face Me in the end, therefore, they must destroy the truth in you. And you are so foolish that you enjoy them and protect them and work to destroy the ones who are Mine.

Who are those who once knew Me and rejected Me? Even the person that was in office that you can't seem to see: he once knew Me and turned on Me. Who is he that he could remain not convicted while you blame someone else for your lack of faith and prayer to bring him to justice? But then Judas knew My Son also and he turned on Him also. You sit seemingly safe now, but when it invades you, then you will understand. You depend on your youth now; you depend on your looks, your ways, your success, your accomplishments, and your abilities; never realizing that in one day that all can disappear. Those of you who claim anyone is unjust have become unjust in order to proclaim it. You become exactly what you claim the other is. You see it within another because it is deep within you. And the only way to see that is to look directly into the mirror of the Word and repent. If you are unjust you will fight and hate to obtain what really doesn't belong to you. If it belonged to you it would have been yours long, long time ago. I would have given it to you gladly. But no, to obtain it without all this hatred and evil thinking is too difficult so you try to obtain it by claiming you, poor you were robbed. I tell you now, you robbed yourself. When you fight against what I have not chosen to remove, who are you fighting against? And if I Am the only One who could remove it, then why do you fight? No soul is converted or changed until I convert them. And if they are not doing what you think is so necessary, why do you get offended if they don't have what you do?

Do you honestly believe that Jesus hated people who were not like Him? What My Son hates are the sins that cause My children to be destroyed; or the sins that take My laws and destroys them. Do you honestly believe that He would approve of what you are doing? If you truly don't make a difference between you and another, then why do you speak of the difference? If you sin and they sin what difference is there? All deny that they are doing that.

The media, all deny that they do this. And all the while they speak about white, black, red, yellow or brown they are all guilty of doing it. And all of you are like little kids in kindergarten pointing out each other's faults as though no one can really see you. As men and as women you play games with the country, the world, and the lives you are to be responsible for. All of you, do these things, not one, but all. When it comes to your national security, I want you to know that this nation is no game. This hour is no game. It is horrible to see that all of those who fight to get so many people that this nation will not be able to handle into it. It is a horrible incident but if the media didn't feed this they wouldn't be so emboldened. But where this will lead to the media and the left will not be able to control it once they unleash this monster.

I don't have to tell you the sins of this nation. What I do have to tell you is to come out of it. Come out of the things that you have allowed to touch your life. The only way out is to come out from it. It has your mind through the media like a trap and lies you don't want free, or you can't get free. But these people are not intelligent. They think their knowledge is power. The only power there is when you have knowledge of Me. And even then these minds play with what little they know so as to never truly do what they need to do in order to be saved.

I Am still stronger than your enemies. Don't permit them to paralyze you with fear. Do n't let them intimidate you to fight. With patience, with wisdom, and understanding; those are the things of your stability; believing that no matter who wants to continue to destroy this nation, I Am not with them. And if I Am not with someone then the end result will be seen. My Word says that you are to keep yourself from the paths of the destroyer. You will never tell Me anything about what a destroyer is and what isn't because I made him. I know that his desire is to kill a person who loves Me and My Word could never kill anyone unless it was in defense of his home, his family or his country. After all, it is only Satan that threatens your nation. It isn't Me. I am not with them. When I see the blood of My Son Jesus Christ I will pass over you. And if I don't see the blood then how can I pass over you? These words are not speaking about war, for there are times that we must go to war and war is always ugly. To defend this great nation some things have to be done in spite of all of her enemies within. Her enemies within give power to all the enemies outside to make this part of the antichrist domain by being global.

The celebrities that take the young are not of Me. It is no marvel that a young person is tempted to be deceived. People who go after the young people know they are taking advantage of the young who do not understand. They know they are deliberately deceiving them and they seek to use them. Don't be deceived. They erase history then got more evil and began touching the children in kindergarten by touching their sex that way they can control them and rape them at will. And out in the open as they have operated for many years they can snub their nose at Me through your help of putting such evil people in office through your vote I will not forget who voted for whole and how you came to your evil conclusions.

If you raised a great young person with the truth, then stand firm in the belief that Satan cannot take them. If you see them striving towards Me and they lack the understanding that you have. Then stand firm in the blood of Jesus to keep them from Satan's clutch. Instead of feeding it by believing that Satan can take what belongs to Me. You raise a young person and teach them all about Me. Then they go to college and some professor who imagines he is something teaches them the opposite of all they have ever learned and it sometimes sticks. But it doesn't need to. You could not imagine the evil that is in some of these colleges. Remember this was exposed how bad many of the colleges are. For years this vessel has been praying for it to be exposed how they take young minds and tell them about alternative lifestyles then teach them how to keep it and stand against all that their parents taught them all of their life and you O foolish one pays for it.

If you are one of the young; know this I will never tear down My order of things. Every person must first be led in order to lead. Every person is led by somebody. Your mind answers the call of whatever you willingly expose yourself to. If you expose yourself to the wrong and then one day you decide to change you forget there are consequences. Those consequences cannot be prayed away. They have to be changed by making them right. By admitting the wrong and making it right with others. They cannot be covered up; they must be dealt with and changed. I erase the sin and forget it after you make it right. The world tells you that it all must be fair and balanced. I tell you plainly to obey My Word and put your moral convictions above those who you think you are going to save. I tell you to know that the moment of conception is life. Life is in the blood. Try and call it a blob of nothing without form if you will but life is in the blood. I will hold everyone responsible who takes life lightly so lightly that they can support someone who gives the right to choose to kill. Midterm elections many of you claiming to be Christian voted to use Congress to hold back a President who would never do these things. Who do you think I will be with. Not you I promise.

If you have ever been at the deathbed of someone and the doctors tell you that they are on life support. That blood is being pumped through their veins and they are going to cut the system off because the brain is dead. Life is not in the brain. It is in the blood. I have raised brain dead people up to prove it. Listen to what was just said about life support systems. The life everyone chooses to destroy so easily will bring something upon your life that you are not prepared to handle. I sent your parents from the time you were little to teach you how to obey the things that I set up. If you read in Romans chapter one how that I wrote in one sentence to obey your parents right alongside with a comma in between, next to the word murder. In order for you to break away, you must murder the spirit of your parents and I don't take that lightly, especially if you were raised in a Christian home, especially if your parents are godly. For I will do all that is within My power to honor your parents who loved you enough to not kill you at birth. It is only My grace that keeps them alive. This isn't a matter of age; this isn't a matter of a difference of opinion. By the year 2012 murder was fastly becoming a matter of opinion. For even today people scream for the life of others never realizing being judged by their own words they seal their own fate according to My word. This is a matter of your life. The blessings you enjoy as a Christian coming from a Christian home came at a great price from your parents. And you honestly believe that I would lead you against that? Because you think you see something in a person, or you heard someone who claims to be Mine or the media say something good about them? If you claim to be Mine then I set up leaders who know My Word, who have lived longer than you and understand far beyond your years. You are capable of making a greater mistake than what you see the elder making. You may be determined to change this country and because you are young you think that you can. I warn you that the change can never be against My Word. If you succeed in helping these devils do it such as those who teach how to destroy through bombing I promise you that you are plotting your own demise eternally.

The desire they have to destroy history is strictly to control the young who has no idea of what was done in the past. The desire to take your protection off of you is to do to you what Hitler did with the Jews. The first thing he did was take away their guns so he could destroy them in death camps. Some of you are so foolish you have no idea of what snake you are following. Professors have turned so many of My young by teaching alternative lifestyles making them revolutionaries taking over their minds with things that will, in the end, destroy them. Being able to work and make a living and choose who you want to help and give is a God-given right by Me. You earned it you do what you chose with it and no protest or March will change the ability that I gave to My people. My Word says if you don't work you don't eat. Yet making and giving it away free lasts only so long. You call yourself a Christian then get into the Bible and find out what that means because people like you are the ones the enemy of your soul uses to destroy a great country. Wake up they want to use you to destroy a country that I gave to you and your ancestors to keep a great people and once they get done with helping their own nation they can then help others in the world. Compassion isn't others first if you destroy your own you can never help others.

I urge you to come to Me and do n't make such a decision without the presence of My Spirit. And I promise you that you will never feel My Presence on the choice to toss away what I taught you in My Word, killing the innocent is murder you must take a stand against it and that stand is by never supporting anyone who believes this is right. I don't say speak out against it, I don't say lift a finger against it. But I do say taste not, touch not, handle not. Come out from among their thinking. Come out from among the agreement with them that they can be the savior of your world. I Am with no one who takes a stand with violence, no one, for no reason could ever turn Me to deliberately destroy someone else. Put things in a proper perspective. If someone breaks into your home and tries to rob your mother and kills her and then rapes your sister is it, Christian, to let them do this? NO! Where has common sense died within the young? You become what you hate. The self-righteousness that lies to you tells you that certain things are alright to do that I will still be with you. I tell you all right now, never! You chose murder when you chose to support someone who thinks nothing of murdering a defenseless person. And if that fact doesn't stir you, then you need to examine your heart in My presence.

People who are in the public eye through music, through movies or any such like don't have a conscience where your life is concerned. If they did, they would never make some of the evil movies that they do. They don't even let their own children watch what they make because they know how evil it is. Like pied pipers, they play a tune to the young. And with smooth talk and a smile, they say nice things, or they know how to speak, how to pretend. And you lift them as high as heaven, and worship the ground they walk on. And when true trouble comes let us see if they can save you, and let us see if they will. When the attraction of their beauty fades where you do suppose they go? Who can help them? They become nothing but has-beens.

And some of you who are older support them because they are either your gender or your ethnic group. And none of you can see how evil this is for you. There are women that I consider Mine that would never touch some of the things that are being done today. There are men who are Mine that would not touch destroying any helpless individual. But you can't see who they are and you know why? You never pay attention to what is going on around you, and when that sweep from the enemy comes you will listen to the individual who can persuade you. Not the one who would ever do things against Me.

I blame those who call themselves by My name and refuse to get into the Word and seek Me. I blame them that the politicians get away with all the lying and cheating and stealing in order to get elected and it seems as if they don't do that, they can't win. I hold a lot of the people accountable to Me for not doing their homework and at the midnight hour expect me to reveal to them who they should choose. If you knew My Word you would see the fruits that destroy innocent babies are not of Me.

It isn't just a matter of praying before you vote. You're like a man who goes to work every day and because he has worked all day he sits like a king after work and tells himself that nothing else should be required of him. He has no real responsibilities, no part in raising the children and being a person who cares not about what goes on in his wife's life or his children's. All he wants to do is come home and play like a little kid. It is with this kind of attitude that people vote. They did their part; all that should be required of them. And many of them pray for their heroes in sports and never pray for their country's condition. And they blame everyone else. Can you see why it is in trouble today? Your responsibility goes far beyond what you think you see that you seem to be accomplishing.

This nation is so bipolar and so opposite one against the other. You have the left called the left and the right called the right for a reason. They are like two powerful magnets that if they face each other they repel each other but if they walked together they would have a powerful pull. That is the condition of the church in so many ways because the leaders to lead the left never desiring to do right. And the right can't compromise on what the LORD has revealed to them they know that it means their salvation is gone. The left has no such thing because they gave up their salvation a long time ago when they turned their back on the truth. So here we are against one another. As Jesus said a country divided against itself can't stand. This was the madness of those who are after globalism. The plan was and is to cause a brother to rise up against brother in order to destroy the whole nation's sovereignty. Then it will be forced into globalism which will usher in the antichrist. That causing brother to rise up against brother happened when three men were called to the former President's White House they came out and made such a racism stir. Knowing the black church was wounded they chose to feed it to destroy them. Not help them. Those leaders could care less about racism they only feed hatred. And people who see themselves as hurt fall for it every time.

It was an easy thing for anyone to do because there are those who live in the past of having false compassion for other countries when all of you must take care of your own first or you won't have a country then what good are you? The past political world is gone. The past safety in the Ten Commandment laws is almost gone. Take heed if you call yourself a Christian. Take heed if you call yourself by My Name which is the Name of My Son. Take heed and listen it isn't too late. Yes, the time will come when the end will come but it is not yet here. And there is a reason for that. I intended to have My children have peace before they come to Me. For them to take the time to see clearly and know exactly how to believe and what to believe and they only way to do that was to send a man like President Trump who believes with all of his heart this nation should and needs to stay sovereign. This is one of the few sanctuaries of those who are Christian. Persecution of the Jews and Christians is infiltrating the whole world. Those of you who refuse to wake up will be caught in the crossfire and be left behind when I call My own. The time to repent is now, and the time to stand up for what and who I Am is now. Not by fighting but by rejecting the left who gives power to the things that you know are wrong. How do you reject them? By voting against them for the wicked wax worse and worse.

PART IX

IS JESUS PRECIOUS TO YOU?

> In the beginning was the Word, and the Word was with God, and the Word was God. The same was at the beginning with God. All things are made by Him, and without Him was not anything made that was made. In Him was life, and the life was the light of men and the light shineth in darkness; and the darkness comprehended it not. (John 1:1-5)

THERE IS A Man whose name is Jesus Christ who is very precious to My heart for He is My Son and I know that all of you think you know how precious that He is to Me, but you don't. And when the time comes to dealing with all these things I will look from heaven and I will see His blood applied to the soul of those who took His Word to their heart and allowed the Holy Spirit to lead, guide and direct them into all truth in the Word. After all, I Am the Spirit of Truth. I do desire those to worship Me in the Spirit and in the Truth. And I warn all of you who claim My name, (you know the name 'Christian?') who claim My Word (you know My Word called the Bible, called the Word in John 1:1?), who claim My Holy Spirit. You know 'The Spirit of Truth.') Get into the Word and read as much as you can of it. Make an achievable goal and read at first a chapter or two a day, and as you get comfortable with that amount, and it becomes a good habit, add a couple more chapters, and when you grow from there, add more. For I make a promise to you right now, that when I come if I don't see the blood of Jesus Christ applied to your heart I will not pass over you. For the blood can only be applied through having the

Word of God written on the tables of your heart. And the only way that can be done is to read it.

This is the message that is going to be preached across the world before I come. This message is very plain, very simple to understand, and the most valuable lesson that you will ever allow yourself to learn. Meditate upon My Word, ponder all the things that I Am saying within those precious pages. Now is the hour in your life that you must use your faith to get the Word within you. Let Jesus live and breathe within you. The New Testament is the beginning of teaching you My will. It has to be a living breathing part of you through living it. Everything else that you will ever understand is not as important as this is to you right now. Look at the Word and see it to be the most important, the most valuable part of your life; look at it as though you can never enter into heaven without knowing it, living it, understanding it, loving it, feeding off of the 'Bread of Life.' Some of you have never lived it; you live only parts of it, the parts that you chose.

As you reject My Words, I will reject you. As you fill your life up with what you so choose within your heart and your soul, so will I fill up your life with what you choose. I will never separate MY Word which is Jesus Christ from the Holy Spirit that I put in the heart of every person who has been converted by accepting Jesus as their personal Savior. You made a commitment to Me when you asked Me to come into your heart. You made a covenant that for some of you, only I kept. I kept My promise and I gave you the Holy Spirit. I kept My covenant and promise and I gave you My Word. I kept My promise and I gave you access to My Throne in the name of Jesus Christ. And many of you never kept your part of the agreement. You still refuse to go into My Word and learn of Me. And My people perish because of their lack of knowledge of Me. You have a vision for this life. That vision is selfish and fulfills your desires if you have not picked up your cross daily and obeyed the Word. I promised that what is not of Me will fall. Look around you. See if I Am with you or not? If you see I Am not, then repent, and trim your lamp with the anointing that can only come in the Word through the power of the Holy Spirit.

You don't understand buying and selling? Did I not say there would be those who would make merchandise of you? Did I not warn you that there would be those who have their own bellies in mind when they persuade you away from My Word and not into My Word? The day truth will come when you will be so foolish as to ask Me 'Did I not prophesy in Your name? Did I not do many wonderful works in Your name? And I will definitely tell you to depart from Me, ye that work iniquity. Because on that day you are so blind that you cannot see that you are coming to Me trusting in the things that you built upon. The things that you think you have done to earn your way into heaven, to earn even prosperity here on earth. To prophecy is what Jesus did, it was not evil. To do many wonderful works and casting out devils are exactly what Jesus did. Why would He call it working iniquity? He calls it that because you depend upon your gifts to get you into heaven instead of depending upon the blood of Jesus Christ. My Holy Spirit's main purpose is to lead you into all truth in the Word; in Jesus. My gift of My Spirit was never intended to prove that you are of Me without ever truly being of Me. You could not imagine how many are depending upon their gift, as though it is the gift that buys your way into heaven when the only way into heaven is the acceptance of Jesus Christ. You say that you can't be gifted without being in Jesus. They do exactly as they chose with their private lives even sin in secret and believe because I use them it is all going to be alright. You call that grace. My grace was never intended to continue in sin. Matthew 1:21 'and she shall bring forth a son, and thou shall call His name JESUS: for He shall save His people from their sins.' It was never intended to take Me in the places that you want to go. My grace was intended to cause Jesus to live so much within you that you could not willfully and deliberately sin against Me. My gifts and calling are without repentance you can use them and still fall from grace. Because you depend upon that gift which you are able to use. That gift was never given for you. It was given to all others. This is why dying daily is so important; you blaspheme so easily. Make Me look like a fool; make Me look like a liar and a cheat. A worker of iniquity is a very special sin. They work against My people, My prophets within the church. They work to do them harm to stop them from being able to do the job I called My people to do. They don't want anyone to be above them they want to be the boss, therefore, they call themselves prophets and apostles without ever being one.

You don't see it, do you? You don't see those who refuse to live the way they ought are still able to do all the things that they had from the beginning of their walk because My gifts are without repentance. So if a preacher steps down off of the pulpit and he beats his wife afterward, he still goes behind the pulpit able to preach or teach. And the whole country of preachers cries out to Me daily as though he is so weak that he can't control himself; they make me look powerless instead of rejecting him. But he's a man of God they say and he is anointed and that makes him special. I say not if he is doing the works of the devil against his own wife. This is no secret this is no mystery. Many of you know of those who have fallen.

What many of you don't know is that because they are able to go on doesn't mean that I am blessing them. It only means that I keep My word, I keep My promise and I will use them at times. But all will have to face Me in the end. True repentance brings true forgiveness. Jesus died to save you from your sins, never to keep you in them. And if you believe that you can't stop sinning as long as you walk on this earth then you do not believe My Word. Because if you die daily to live My Word Jesus would be so powerful in you, that you could never do the things that you do now. Power is first given to repent and heal the spirit within you enough to be a usable vessel. But it costs so much to die daily for you that you receive the deception and think that you will enter into heaven...

It is easier to say that we all sin in some way every day. A heart that loves Me, My Word and My Spirit can never do that. There is not a sin, no matter how evil, no matter how seemingly small that can't be overcome. You were to overcome it all in you first, then teach others how to live like Jesus. I Am not speaking of every person who claims My name. If you are not doing these things, if you don't willfully and deliberately accept that you have to sin, then happy are ye. Keep those things that I have taught you. To all others, I say repent. Cry out to Me to be free and I will set you free. That cry from the beginning of your salvation journey was to continue until it was finished, for I Am the author and the finisher of your faith. And the beginning continues until the end.

I told you plainly to eat My flesh and drink My blood. The Word is all the blood of Jesus Christ, and the Word is also all of the 'Bread of Life' which is Jesus Christ and yet many of you have put it on a shelf and left the ability to understand it in another's hands. You will listen to every false doctrine, every lying creature because you don't want to come to Me and repent and be what you ought to be. You needed to read it yourself. You needed to pray for yourself. You needed your personal relationship with Me. Not depending on anyone else to get it for you, or give it to you. This was, and is, and has been between you and Me.

This gift of the Holy Spirit which was given to you was given to lead you into the Word and cause the Word to abide within you. Through you, each and every one of you I intended to do many mighty miracles to see many souls saved. So many of you are satisfied with what little you have and as Paul said, you turned to weak and beggarly things. You run to others to intercede for you when there is only one mediator between God and man and His name is Jesus Christ. As long as the flesh is abiding in you then you corrupt everything that I intended for you. The Holy Spirit was to operate through you, without ever being hindered, and the only purpose for that was to give glory to Jesus Christ. That is the only way that I can abide within you.

If you put the Word off daily, you put My Son off daily. And the time will come when you will want to play 'catch up' and it will be too late, so I Am telling you now that all the self-help books, all the preaching, and teaching can't put that personal relationship with Jesus Christ within you, the only way you can have it is by living on the 'Bread of Life', not by reading little pieces of Him daily to accomplish your desires. Living means just that, living within you. Oh, you say that He is your personal savior, and you tell everyone about it. You lift up your hands towards heaven and ask Him to come into your heart, and when the time comes to know Him in His Word you put Him in His place in your life, on a shelf. Most of you do this, except when you want something, and then you put that part in you. The time is at hand to repent of these things, especially those of you who claim to be My prophets

So I ask you plainly, I plead with you in My love, in the love that I had for you so much that My Son died to take you into heaven with Him; I ask you to repent of giving glory to anyone but the One who died for you. For I promised you that every knee shall bow, every tongue confesses that Jesus Christ is LORD. Do you understand that a Lord rules, reigns, and controls you? And if Jesus hasn't done that through His Word in you, it is because you would not put Him in there to do so, and then ask yourself a question where are you? And who are you following? Think about all the years that I gave you upon this earth with the opportunity to put the

Word into your heart and your mind. Think about how many times I sent someone to preach and teach and you felt you didn't have to because you were wrapped safely and securely in your religion or in a ministry. And your religion doesn't have the power to take you into heaven neither does your ministry.

Some of you have the audacity to tell Me that you know what My Word says. You read it and you now know everything. There is only one way. Jesus said 'I Am the Truth, the Life, and the Way. No man can come to the Father but by Me.' But you listened to someone who claimed they read the Word and you accepted what they said even when it went against the words that were deliberately written in red to stand out so that you would have no excuse. They were quotes of Jesus Christ and those words say 'In vain do they worship Me teaching doctrines of men'.

When you are taught that once you give your life to Jesus that you are always in Jesus no matter what you do, that you can't lose your salvation, you need to go into the Word and read in Hebrews that you can lose your day of grace by tramping on the blood of Jesus Christ, and that it is a fearful thing to fall into the hands of the Living God for doing so? That experience of Me holding this vessel in my hand in eternity to prove this part of believing you can do anything and still be saved is a lie. It backs up what Hebrews said about trampling on the blood of Jesus by continuing in sin. read and think again. Or did you take what someone else told you that it all said? How foolish it is that? You didn't search it out for yourself? What a chance you take with eternity. You come close to tramping on His blood when you count the Word as nothing. When you do this in ignorance, and I come and tell you, then you need to let Me begin to work with you to help you face up to your response to the Word. Never did I intend for you to take comfort in being able to count My Son's blood as something so worthless and powerless that you can't cease from sin, or want to. Jesus' own words were that none were lost that God the Father gave Him except for the son of Perdition. And that son of perdition walked with Him and then turned on Him so if it was impossible it would have never happened.

Look at your hands and where do they go? Look at your feet where do they go? When I said if your hand offends you cut it off. You are so foolish that I must not have meant that. The cutting off isn't a physical thing. Whatever you are into that causes your hand to sin, you are to cut that out of your life. How swiftly do they run to shed innocent blood? Do you run to tell everyone what your neighbor seems to be doing? Do you run to spread things to make yourself look good and another look evil? Look at your heart and see where it has been. How swiftly does it judge and condemn your brother? I said to be swift to hear and slow to speak, but I never said be swift to hear or see what another is doing so that you can be swift to judge someone. Therein is My hatred for brother rises up against brother and devours one another and calls it a blessing from Me. And you are so foolish that you think this is what I intended when I made this nation great to glorify Me.

This nation was not made great because of the people who formed it. Although many were Mine and their obedience to Me was and is their greatness. It was made great because it is the only nation who always stood with Israel. There were those who read the Word and believed the Word and obeyed the Word. I promised that I would bless those who blessed Israel and that I would curse those who cursed Israel. And because in your flesh you have not seemed to see the blessing or the curse it is no matter to Me. I do exactly as I chose with what belongs to Me. I chose them, just as I chose the true believing Christian. I called them, just as I called those who love My Son. And if you become offended with these facts then I suggest you read the Word, for they say a word for word what is being written here in this book. I ordained it, I decided it, I will bring all things to performance according to My Word and no one will change it no matter what it looks like now, or has looked like. I said that I chose you; you did not choose Me. Peter confessed that Jesus is the Son of the Living God. Jesus told him plainly that flesh and blood did not reveal that to him. It came directly from the My Throne, so if you believe that Jesus Christ is My Son and that I raised Him from the dead then I personally revealed that to you. I personally chose you to belong to My Son.

The floodgates have opened and hell has enlarged herself. And My angels are ready with their sickles. Come out, My children. Come out from anything, or anyone who leads you to believe one thing against My Word. Remain with those who faithfully and honestly and truthfully have told you what is in the Word and warned you to get into it and obey My Son. For today is the day of salvation. Today is the day unlike any other. For the time is short and no games will be played, I Am right now drawing a line. I Am right now writing in My book those who obey and those who refuse. You will not see it in the flesh. You will not hear it in the flesh. But those who are Mine will see and hear.

I Am not speaking about what your leaders have told you that My Word says. I Am speaking about you getting into the Word where you learn, not religion. Not church history and lie that it is the only true church and if you don't belong to it, and obey its doctrine then you are not going to make heaven. Let it be known today Any church that dares teach or preach if you are not of them that you are not with Christ is a cult. For they preach another gospel, another way to be saved. If they tell you at any time that because you wear your hair a certain way or you wear makeup, or if you play cards or anything such like that you are going to hell doesn't believe them because they didn't die for you. Because they pay so much attention to the outside of the vessel they pay no attention to the things within the heart that matters before Me. Many things are so harmless and you can make a sin out of them. To the pure all things are pure. Don't you see how easy it is to be deceived? Take the weightier matters and work with them. I promise you today that if you don't belong to My Son Jesus Christ through having His blood applied to your sins, you have no part in Me. Read My Word, no one has the power to forgive you of sin except Jesus Christ, because no one else died for you. No one can cause you to pay penance for your sins. No amount of praying, no amount of anything can ever erase your sin except asking God for the blood of Jesus Christ to erase it by forgiving you.

And I warn you don't twist this up to mean that if you wear pants and you are a woman that you are not of Me if you wear makeup and you are a woman that you are not of Me. I taught in My word to dress modestly, that means to cover your body. You taught and believed in extremes in clothing, hair etc. You taught that the skirts have to be down to the floor and the neckline has to be up to the neck. I didn't teach that no man has a right to condemn you or tell you that you are not welcome in church. If you are so ignorant that you dress almost naked and expose your breasts or your thighs then the sin is yours, repent; these things are paid so much attention to, that it takes away from the truth of the gospel. If you are preaching against religions, against people, against anyone, then you are not preaching the gospel. My church needs to be taught how to allow Jesus to live within their hearts and minds.

While you were busy deciding things like wearing pants, a woman not having roles in the church there are many souls that were being destroyed in this country. While you busy yourselves with things that have no real meaning such as women not being able to preach children were being destroyed because the most important things were being neglected while you fought over nothing. Children were raped looking for a savior, their own parents turning on them and you were too busy for Me to call into intercessory prayer. You were fighting over nothing.

PART X

THE SON OF PERDITION

And as they did eat, He said Verily I say unto you, that one of you shall betray Me. And they were exceeding sorrowful and began every one of them to say unto him, Lord, is it I? And He answered and said, he that dippeth his hand with Me in the dish, the same shall betray Me. (Matthew 26:21-22)

While I was with them in the world, I kept them in Name: those that Thou gavest Me I have kept and none of them is lost, but the son of perdition, that the scripture might be fulfilled. (John 17:12)

Let no man deceive you by any means: for that day shall not come, except there come a falling away first, and that man of sin be revealed, the son of perdition.
(II Thessalonians 2:31)

THESE MEN WERE His apostles and they walked and talked, and lived and breathed their life with Him. They heard things that we have yet to hear. They were given understanding and truths that we still have yet to learn. And yet every one of them said to Him 'Lord, is it I?' They had the Word every day with them. They walked with Him and listened to Him for hours, days and years. And yet at that moment, none knew their own heart. Each one at times had to be told and explained in detail the parables. He questioned them, asking are they yet without understanding? Still, after all this time that He spent with them;

are they still without understanding? He didn't get angry with them. He didn't hate them, He didn't punish them, but He most certainly did deal with them. He knew that the consequences of their own actions would be punishment enough. The LORD waits for you to see and repent from your wicked ways but there comes a day that if He wants you to make heaven you force His hand to have to deal with you. When time after time you do not listen then He has to do something to keep you from jumping off of a cliff to hell.

I AM called "God The Father" for a reason. I AM Father. When your child is warned over and over to not do something or touch something or told not to go anywhere that might hurt them. You as a fleshy father may sit there in the same room when they are young and tell them over and over not realizing how many times you have told them not to. Then suddenly you get so fed up that you don't take anymore. Maybe if it is dangerous you don't want someone to get hurt. Or if it is just plain irritating that they won't listen or pay attention to you, after all, you are their father. Either way or whatever the reason you suddenly decide that is enough and you get up. You then move and do something about it. Perhaps you spank them or stop them in some way but either way you do something about it; you move. Well, I AM GOD the Father and when you move Me out of My place My word warns you that I AM a terrible God then. For since I AM God I will make the decision that it will take to stop the whole thing and it won't matter how you feel about it. If you like it; don't like it or if it hurts real bad it doesn't matter to Me. I warned you over and over not to touch, not to do.

When you saw that Peter wept because he denied Jesus three times, were you able to see how Peter must have felt? Peter would have rather died than to be found doing this, but it happened because Peter did not know what was in his own heart at that time. Jesus knew. Even when the truth hurt, He spoke it plainly and clearly lest any of you should misunderstand.

Are you going to now be wise enough to ask 'Lord is it I?' Every one of you that have not the Word abiding in you is capable of betraying Me. In an hour that you are sure that you will not deny Me, you can and perhaps will just like Peter. Peter was positive that he would never betray Jesus, but he did, and so will you if you don't fill up with the Word. Today protect your soul, protect your vessel, and protect yourself through the Word.

When you have Jesus Christ within, in the Word; the word rises upon the occasion of temptation that you need to overcome everything. How can He resurrect in you and keep you the way He promised if you will not ever let Him in?

I have heard many preach and teach and talk about those who walked with My Son or talked with Him in the Garden and each time it was with so little respect. Not realizing that any one of you is capable of betraying Me without My Word within you. Hear what I Am going to say and don't say it to anyone as though I said this is speaking of any particular person. Because right now at this moment I Am the only person who knows who is the son of perdition spoken of in the book of in the Word.

Everyone wonders if the Anti-Christ is living on the earth today. They look for signs and they don't realize that they are looking in all the wrong places. According to the scriptures, he has to emerge after walking and talking with Jesus the way Judas did. He will know Jesus Christ intimately and then turn on Him. In order to betray Me, he will know a lot about Jesus. I Am not telling you that he will know a lot about religion. I am saying that he will know a lot about Jesus. He will have walked and talked with My disciples. He will be convinced in the end that he knows better than what he was taught of Me. He will turn slowly the way Judas did and ripen for the hour. He will betray Jesus for money the way Judas did. He will have been in on everything that God was doing and then go to those who thought they were in control and betray Jesus by telling all he heard and knew in order to destroy Jesus and His disciples. Very much like the man who got into office and led everyone to understand all about the true believer and how to betray them. How to capture them and make sure they never get elected. And just think; you helped him when you voted for him and you help him even now when you refuse to accept the only one that I sent.

Remember this O Christian that I AM saying this to you this day. I will never send another after him. He is the one I chose; he is the one I will and do work with and I don't care if you like him or don't. I AM GOD and he will not pay for the evil that you have done to him and to your country by not supporting him and listening to every lie in the hateful media. I can wipe them out, but I won't. Not until I AM done judging you who call yourself by My Name because judgment begins in the house of God and if the righteous scarcely be saved where will the sinner and ungodly appear?

Believe Me or not a lot of this has already taken place with some antichrists. This vessel wrote a handwritten letter to every big named preacher who had the power to warn the church if they would. Did they warn you? Or did they send her a letter and tell her that it gives them the power to see what they will be used against them when the time comes. The time came when I spoke through that letter and they should have believed Me that I would send someone to hold things off so that more could come in but they didn't do that. In their self-righteousness they said within themselves that God says this is supposed to come to pass so for them it was written in stone. But I had a greater plan than what their little minds contrived.

You see, I revealed to this vessel what was going on with the people who once knew Christ and turned on Him. They began to gather up all the information that was taught by big named preachers (who were not supposed to give that which is holy unto those who did not know Me.) But these big named preachers bought and sold Bible verses; bought and sold the word until finally their enemies and the enemies of the Lord in this nation had all they thought they needed to deliver you into the arms of Satan. And you as a parishioner fed it all and supported it all. You still have time to correct it by supporting your President. You could clearly see that when the IRS scandal came out one of the most important things they wanted to know was how did the Republicans pray? Now, why would they want to know that?? Well, they wanted to use what they had learned from those who bought and sold the gospel to defeat the Christian at their own level of understanding. They planted Rhinos to pretend they were of the same party to fight them and you voted them in office. Please for your sake get on your knees and pray that you not only be forgiven for the things that you are personally responsible for but pray for the nation and the church not to be blessed but to be led to repentance as you are led to repentance that all may be forgiven before I come. Do you remember one of My so-called preacher's teaching that you are unstoppable in Christ? Well, do you also remember one of the enemies within this nation telling the world that they were unstoppable? They took all that My children taught to the masses and turned it around on My children. And they were defeated enough to have a godless person use all they taught against them to defeat them. Even today it seems to effectively work in some cases. What was supposed to happen to the devils was their world be turned upside down. But due to the weakness of the church through sin, they were able to turn this nation upside down and make wrong right and right wrong and they did it right in front of you because while the media distracted you and worshipped this evil couple you let them and listened and obeyed their opinions. Not the news but their opinions. And you loved it because they in the spiritual realm of evil know exactly how to make you feel like you and they are the only two that have intelligence.

And you forgot My word that said with man's wisdom he did not know God nor did he think he needed God. So God chose the foolishness of preaching for the only way to be saved. The adulteresses and adulterers tell you daily that you and they are the only adults in the room. And you fell for it. You forgot that you should have rather been a fool for Christ sake than be used by the devil for one moment. A young woman was found dead in the office of a Congressman who gets to tell you daily that he is an adult and Trump is not. Just like the one that let a girl drown and he got to sit in judgment of other people. This is the kind of people that you listen to trash your President daily. It turns the stomach.

My Son Jesus NEVER taught the masses and never told them that all of them were called to be ministers. He taught those that He called out and called them His apostles and taught some alone. Not the masses. Listen to what I Am saying. Those children that you work so hard outside this country to feed while you let those within this country starve have it all mixed up. Only an anti-Christ spirit could turn on the LORD and reveal how to defeat My children. The only one who has the LORD could lead them out of these things. He wanted to do it by draining the swamp of hell that festered and infected this nation against the LIVING GOD. If you belong to Jesus you do have an anointing a calling. It takes the Holy Spirit to answer the call of being a mother, father, sister, brother, friend, daughter, son and Aunt, Uncle etc. This is why you have father's raping daughters and sons because they do not have Me inside of them they are soulless and don't know the difference between right or wrong and don't care they only lust for evil. All can only be good at what they do if they have the Holy Spirit; just like it takes an anointing to be the President of the United States. And if a mother is called and anointed to be a mother she is making herself ineffective and will answer if she decides she doesn't want the baby. Only Christian woman is worse they desert their babies and blame Me and lie they are saving souls and I told them to desert their own. Not so. Even if she goes out and preaches the gospel and is used in missionary work doesn't mean that I called her that way. I can even use her but she will answer for the ones she left behind.

The son of Perdition will be a pretender in his heart and find no real value in the Word even though he claims to have it. He will have the right words, at the right time, and know how to act, how to overcome, how to do things to appear as though he has Jesus Christ within him. He will even on occasion confess Jesus. He will have no passion in his heart for anyone or anything but him. He will be sure that he knows it because he has read it and sat under preaching that looks and sounds so much like the truth. He will have belonged to a ministry that is as self-seeking as he is. It will be so close that only Mine will see it. Mine will know the hour that it turns; they will see it just before it happens. Just as Jesus knew which one was going to betray Him, those that have Jesus within them will know who he is. He will not be a man of religion. He will claim to know salvation. He will slowly see himself as a Savior. At first, he will think that he is of Me. Then the power within his hands will corrupt him the way Satan was corrupted by his own beauty and power. Any other man could be put in power and this never happens. This could not happen to any other man on earth. Only this one would take it the way he does and will.

Listen to what I tell you. There are many anti-Christs, and they all begin with some knowledge of Me through the knowledge of the Word. And they break out of the Word and make everything the way they want. They will be self-seeking, and very able to accomplish it. And this is done even today in so many ways. Many of those ways are spoken about constantly in this book. Self, self, self, centeredness finally took Judas. This man will take everything as though it belongs to him. At first, he will not know who he is, that is why it will not be revealed until the time. Judas didn't know until the time. I Am the only One who knows the time. Listen to what I Am saying here. Listen that this will be a man who is so corrupt in his soul that he can claim to be Christian when in reality he believes in another god. His aim will be to destroy this nation and every Christian.

Your President's aim is to destroy the atrocities in this nation I called him to this. The evil one is one who will fight to keep the evil going on for he will be filled with the devil and able to deceive the ignorant. Those who allowed the media tell them who is who and what is what for years following this person. All I am saying is this is his personality to destroy this nation because it is and was Christian. He will fight against the Christian so that he can remain in his hidden evil. Remember ALL this was written in 2007 and now it is 2018.

He will have no regard for women. Some men like men and not women even though they are married. Many of My kings loved beautiful women but this man will have no regard for them. He could be married. Because it could perhaps only means that he accepts no woman as having the power or the right to preach or be able to pastor, or to be a leader of any organization or nation. He will not consider what they think or feel. It could mean that he thinks a woman's place is in the home taking care of her children and that I would never use her as a prophet, as a leader of any country. Consider what I am telling you! Those of you who know the Word will know what I am saying. Your headship as a man gives you power over your wife to rebuke the enemy and protect her from any onslaught against your family and you're calling which includes her. I made no man lord over his wife. I gave him no power to dictate to her how she should serve Me when I call her. I gave no man special permission to mistreat her, or abuse her verbally, or to abuse her by treating her as though she is so much less than he. I did clearly say that her body is yours and your body is hers. Never did I say that you were to take My Son's place over her with her calling. Ask yourself, do you honestly believe that a man is greater than a woman? Or do you know that I make no difference just as I make no difference with color, where you live, or even your church if it is preaching the gospel? If you line up with Me then I line up with you. When I say I make no difference I mean no difference; I don't call them because they are one color in particular, or came from a suffering hardship culture, or gender. I Am no respecter of persons.

Everyone who obeys My Word is the same to Me. And if you claim Me, remember a past is not something that you simply brush under the rug and pretend nothing ever happened and believe that I will cover it for you. It is something that you work out by repenting of it and that takes admitting you did what you did. You can never say it is personal just between you and Me if you ever hurt anyone including an innocent child. Remember only by confessing (admitting your sin) and taking it to the Throne and acknowledging Jesus is the only way for you to be saved and get into heaven. That Jesus is the only reason that you have access to My Throne; that Jesus rose from the dead to break the power of death over all those who all their life feared death. That He rose from the dead and went into heaven to prove this.

This vessel sat in the pew of a church and saw two huge angels striving against one another. Each one was taking a stand. One strove and shoved against the other. They strove very hard to push one another off of their stand. Each shove was felt within her. One would seem to gain ground but the feet were firmly planted so like two wrestlers they could only shove. She sat there unable to cry, unable to pray and even after the experience unable to speak to any person about it for many years. Because up until today (which is July 20, 2007); she did not understand what she saw. (Now it is 2018 and she understands) Her mouth was bound unable to speak; her hands were bound behind her back unable to use them in prayer. She strove so hard to be free. It almost took her physical life, and it almost took her soul for she could feel both the physical life almost die and the spiritual life at the brink. And there was nothing that she could do; she did not know what to do. Even though she suffered tremendously just watching it, she could see herself bound and gagged. And now she realizes that it was the Jesus within her that was bound and gagged by the church. That struggle was a fight for the pulpit. Not the pulpit of that particular church but the church. Brother against brother, each one claiming that I Am with them.

Are you so foolish even now to think that all of this is written against My church? No, this is written for My church. The light has been turned on, not for others to see, but for you in your personal relationship with Me. Never would I reveal even one truth in this book if I did not intend to protect you, keep you, strengthen you, and help you to not only overcome but be more victorious in your life than you ever have been before. Never do I ever reveal anything that seems negative in a warning without showing you the way out. Never would I ever speak so harshly seemingly at times if it wasn't for the fact that some of you need it so much. Anything I say to you is for you to use as an opportunity to get it all right. Never to make you get so low with it that you cannot get up. It is never to condemn you, but only to convict you. Because I have a place for you all planned out and it is a place that you will want to be with Me. I have a plan for you and it is not for evil but for good for you. My arms are open wide waiting for you to come to Me. If you know all these things then as the scripture says 'happy are ye.'

This church that she saw this war it had a spirit that was released within it. She doesn't remember the exact occasion but she will never forget what she felt. I told her that it was a Judas spirit. It had a tremendous impact; she could feel it so strongly. Put it in the light of the warring angels and this release, and you can understand it. There was no reason that it manifested; because it was for one purpose to be recognized, only to be seen as to what it was. No such thing as rebuking this spirit. Some things you can pray all day long and if they are ordained by Me then I Am not looking for you to rebuke it. What I Am looking for is for you to obey the Word through it. Dying to self is your only path to freedom, through obedience to Jesus Christ. You must die to yourself and let Jesus live. It can never work if you only think you know Who Jesus is; remember I said this for this is important to your soul. You must know Him.

And most of all, this woman never even to this day pray any other way but 'Thy will be done'. And she never presumes what that will is. Only in My Presence will she receive any word. And only in My Presence will she pray knowing it is safe to pray. Those of you who have the Spirit of God within you will ask, is it I Lord, because it will be clear that you may not know your own heart and this is why this hour it is very important to know it enough to pray. To ask if there be anything within you that doesn't belong and be willing to accept the fact that if there is and you recognize it; then it isn't you. You can seek forgiveness and repent.

Notice that none of them ever asked Jesus which one; they asked Him is it I? Therefore they knew and understood that He would never talk about anybody to them. He did not say one word until the time. And that was only because he wanted them to see it when it came to pass and to pray for Him. Hear what I am saying. Stop and pray over this. It is a true revelation. The abomination that makes desolate is something that makes the soul desolate. And nothing makes the soul more desolate than rejecting the Word which is Jesus, claiming Jesus and having some other god to get into heaven.

Remember what I told you about soulless people. They are people who have no sense of what is right or wrong through My Word, My Spirit or My children. From the time they are born into this world they are already filled with evil because some mother rubbed their belly daily and chanted "Kill Jews" Or "Kill Americans". As they are rubbing on the belly comforting the baby within with comfort from the words "Kill, kill, and kill." Remember what Jeremiah said how that I knew Jeremiah before he was born; before he came out of his mother's womb.

Is the other way for you the doctrine of your church that teaches women can't preach or teach? Is the doctrine of your Christ that if you do play a game of cards or if you do wear makeup, or if you dance you are going to hell? Is that your doctrine that if you make a sign something that means nothing tells you that person is going to hell? I that your doctrine; because if that is your doctrine then you are preaching and teaching another doctrine other than the doctrine of Christ which is the only true doctrine.

Because Jesus died for them and He knows exactly where their heart is and you can't reach in there and destroy what He is doing under the shadow of His wing with them. You have tossed out Christ and let your doctrine or church body live in His place. Wake up. No one can tell another person they are going to hell because they don't belong to your church. Is your church the one that lets every devil in hell play with witchcraft and let them take the name of Jesus everywhere in evil to blaspheme Him every day of their lives? Is your doctrine the one that dares to take My place and makeup all the rules and regulations and tradition of a church body? And you leave My Son out. The price He paid means nothing? Are you the one that goes into other nations and betrays your own nation by feeding them what you think is the gospel giving them the power to destroy this nation? Is that your doctrine? I can go on and on. Telling you exactly this there is NO other way to be saved meaning there is NO one who can damn you to hell either. You work out your own salivation between you and God.

There is a line of demarcation that I have drawn. YES. That line definitely says if you do a certain thing that you are following the enemy of your soul. And it does say that the way is straight and narrow. But I have no men the power to determine the heart of other men and women who do not know what you know. Until I the LORD lead you and tell you what is going on I say judge nothing until the LORD comes for a reason. Many of My children are being destroyed before they even come out of the womb in salvation because of these false doctrines that kill rather than save.

Or taking a part of what He did say in the Word and taking it as your own. Watch and pray over your own soul that you not be taken. If your religion tells you that you are going to hell if you don't belong to their religion then you are listening to another gospel. And My Word definitely curses any other gospel. The war she saw was a war for the pulpit. One side would not and did not have the Word; therefore they did not live the Word. They only claimed it. The other side wanted the Word but did not know how to obey the Word. I tell you even know the truth many of you do not know how to obey the Word because you never go into the Word and you let your leaders tell you what it means.

The Anti-Christ will come in his own name. He will be a great communicator. He will seem to bring so much peace and hope and many will look upon Him as a savior. (this part already took place with a certain group of people who thought he was their savior and I would deliver those who labored hard all their lives into their hands that refused to work.) His ability to speak to all nations will be phenomenal. (That has been done they all lined up to global warming and globalism.) You know why he will have this power? Because he is not of me and neither are many other nations. The world loves its own. He will seem to have the answer to many problems; be able to speak to all others in other nations that have always hated and distrusted the West because of jealousy that I blessed America not them. And he will seemingly become all things to all men so that he can accomplish his will, to his purpose, to his agenda. At first, he will appear very righteous, and what knowledge he has in that righteousness will appear very genuine because he really doesn't know. Inside of his heart, he will never reveal who he really is. He will seem to be a Christian. He will seem to have some righteousness or at least the ability to reach out to God.

Right now this day if you look at this you will see clearly that this is a man who sat for years under the gospel. One who had enough knowledge the way Judas did. Judas walked and talked with the LORD for the years Jesus had His ministry. This one will walk and talk with God for many,

many years. Not one, not two, not even ten but many years and in those years he had always denied My Son; he never loved him and chose another god because he thought he knew better than Myself. Chose an evil god that blasphemed Me, My word, and the country that I chose the way I chose Israel. His hatred didn't come from his race being persecuted; it came from an inner savage hatred for anyone or anything other than himself to be lifted up. This is what you become in the end when you decide that you don't want My Son anymore. When you want to have it all for yourself.

Hitler had this kind of power to persuade so many people, to sweep across his nation and convince them to destroy the Jews. The worst atrocities were committed because destroying another human being was so easily accepted. He killed Jewish babies also and experimented with all kinds of people with animals etc. He had no soul. Like I said to have a soul you have to have the law of God written in your heart to know the line of demarcation that My laws draw between good and evil. He had no respect or honor for the elderly. He rose up an army of young people because the young are easy to deceive because they don't have the knowledge that can only be obtained by experience through knowledge of history. This is why they have to destroy history because of wanting to control the young. If the young know nothing about the past they will follow the same paths that were done before the same mistakes will be repeated.

This man who came before this President hates the sovereignty of this country because his aim is to use the world to control the world. Listen carefully to what I say, because for a long time it will not be seen until it is time to manifest. Just as Judas went to sup with Jesus and dipped his bread, so shall this man. And by the time you see him manifest, it may be too late. This will be something that will never be revealed until the time. It can only be seen by God's children who are filled with the Holy Spirit, filled with the Word of God Jesus, and filled with My will. The world right now is ripe to worship anyone. You can see it in the young, how they worship at their concerts. How people worship celebrities. He will have been with Jesus long enough to have learned how to handle himself and how to say all the right things in order to appear to be what he is not. And then suddenly he will turn. Whether he is on the earth today is unimportant because it will only come to pass when it is time. It will never be seen until that moment that I choose to manifest it.

Remember that Judas didn't do one thing until the time appointed. Picture the scene in your mind. He kept silent as he walked and talked with Jesus and His disciples. He never revealed what was truly working within him. Don't deceive yourself into thinking that anyone knew until the moment that it happened. This is why My Word says that they asked 'Is it I Lord", Judas's closest associates did not know until the moment. This is why no one right now knows the time or the hour all these things will happen. Many of you will not understand what I am saying here, but all who are Mine will. And many of you will be tempted to believe even now that you see him, here or there. I tell you I have not revealed him yet and I will reveal him to Mine, not all of you who claim to be Mine are Mine. You must have the Word abiding in you to be Mine. Many of you think because you are with Me that you are entitled to know ahead of time, but this is not according to My Word. The son of perdition is the only one appointed to be lost. Listen to what I Am saying, and ponder on the truth of these Words.

His persuasion will be very powerful, at first, it will seem as though I Am with him because of his ability to persuade through speech. The only way you will know him is by examining his fruits, and never by his words. I have told you many times that there are many anti-Christs in the world so don't deceive yourselves into believing that you know who I Am speaking about. I will let you know in the appointed time. His fruits are evil enough to destroy the innocent babies through abortion. That is one big sign. His evil will be enough to change the nature of things in the man or woman that I created. Hitler did those things. He will defy all law that tells him that it is the law of God he is against. He will work to destroy the law in this country and give permission to destroy and make murder a matter of opinion. Hating will be his robe of whatever he wants to call it. He will strive to cause hatred enough to obtain power.

You don't want it and yet you still claim it. I call that crazy! The whole time people who claim Me fight against the truth of My Spirit My ways in others and demand for accountability to come to those who are obeying the truth by denying Satan the power to destroy babies, or using little ones for their pleasure. All that time they are having gatherings and having prayer meetings and used those meetings to celebrate the right to kill the baby inside of them. Persecuting and hating the truth in My children. Making it impossible for them to choose who they want to vote for by hurting them. To these people I Am dead, but to My people, Jesus, the Holy Spirit and Myself are very much alive. From My Throne, I Am watching and I keep good books and remember I Am not blind. I see all the atrocities. No man can call them anything else. Even the invasion of this nation will wind up an atrocity if they are not stopped. Ask Me to prevent their take over to hold back the time for a season to get more in of My children in Christ with the truth; for the truth will set you free.

PART XI

ARE YOU POSITIVE HE'S NOT COMING YET?

> Therefore be ye also ready: for n such an hour as ye think not the Son of man cometh. (Matthew 24:44)

MY SON PROMISES to come upon you as a thief in the night. As I have told you before that I do visit you and will take away what you seem to have so that all that remains is what is of Me and you will have to work and struggle your way back. But this scripture is speaking about My coming when you are sure that I Am not coming back the way I said that I would.

Luke 17:20-24 'And when He was demanded of the Pharisees when the kingdom of God should come, He answered them and said, The kingdom of God cometh not with observation: Neither shall they say, Lo here! Or, lo there! For, behold the kingdom of God is within you. And he said unto the disciples, 'The days will come when ye shall desire to see one of the days of the Son of man, and ye shall not see it.' And they shall say to you, See here; or, see there: go not after them, nor follow them. For as the lightning that lightened out of the one part under heaven shineth unto the other part under heaven; so shall also Son's returns be in His day.'

Do you understand what He is talking about how the Kingdom of God is within you and how it is going to shine from one end of heaven to the other? How He had said that we will recognize Him when He comes for we will be like Him and if we are not like Him then how can we recognize Him? There is a section in this book about how the prisoners were released and as far as the eyes could see that many prisoners were released but only one recognized Jesus when He came. That she and she alone touched Him. If all of you repent that read this book and get on your knees and determine that you will not do one thing to glorify Satan anymore in your life and that you will glorify the LORD Jesus Christ. The shine in the hearts of everyone who belongs to Him would be tremendous.

I have told you about this vessel writing this book how someone came to her home and her husband came to pick her up and the woman wanted to introduce him to her. And he stood there and covered his eyes as you would from the sun. And said, "I can't, I can't, she is too bright." How that when she went to go get her license picture taken how the woman taking the picture came out and said, "I could not capture an image it was so bright, so light that I had to turn the camera on all the way to get an image."

The words in this book are the words that will enlighten you to get ready for the rapture. They are what I want revealed for the time is at hand to be ready, and if I do not deal with you here, you will never be ready to go with Jesus. Take a look at this scripture, ask yourself why would I say that they shall say see here or see there? Why would I tell you to go not after them? The kingdom of God is within you. Why do you run everywhere to find Him? He is right there in your home, with you in the Word, with you in the Spirit. Why do you run everywhere to find Him? You need healing He is within you. You need to be delivered, He is within you. I will tell you why, because you have not done what you are supposed to do according to My Word to allow the kingdom of God to prosper within you.

Let understanding enter. Just as I have told you about the foolish virgins how they were unspotted from the world that is why they were called virgins. Yet Jesus Christ rejected them. The story the preachers tell is that it is because knowing the word they rejected the Spirit and to a point that is true. But the complete truth is they rejected the Anointing that can ONLY be found in the reality of the word written in the heart of every believer. Forcing the word in there by memorization, by study, by the school does not make you Mine. It makes you a scholar and this vessel writing these words the first thing she will tell you is that she is not a scholar. Yes, she did try to take a Bible college course after I told her not to because the Holy Spirit taught her. Her teacher never knew what I revealed to her and her heart was broken by many scholars that she thought were men of God real pastors and found they were liars. All of them; not one, not two but all were found to be liars. She is not a scholar and she never learned it by study and memorization. She learned it by walking and talking with a close relationship with Jesus Christ for many years. For many years where only My Son spoke to her night and day and she listened and did not pray or speak back as the anointing of Jesus Christ filled every atom of her being.

You can hear those preachers say that what the others learned in thirty years they obtain in one day. Perhaps true but this you can't learn by reading or studying. This you can't just pick up and see what they did and imitate them and pray for you to be like them. This is Christ and He won't be imitated He demands complete and absolute service. Complete and absolute obedience to His will. What are you going to do now with all of your millions what have you obtained? Ask yourself did you obtain a relationship with My Son? Or what someone else told you or taught you?

JUST CONSIDER THIS: I will not come in the wind, I will not come in the rain, and I will not come in the snow, for I need nothing within the earth to deal with you. I will not come to another person. I will not come in a storm; I most definitely will come within the temple that you dwell in. I will come to you. The terror will be within a man's soul and a place where only he knows exists, but more importantly a place where only I know all things. In your very being, you will feel it. Where you have played with My words, where you have played with all of life and souls, I will most definitely visit within you. Those who are obedient, and have come to ask Me if they are where they need to be and My Presence confirmed it shall be very blessed for them on that day.

I am going to visit everyone within himself or herself. Listen to what I say! I am not saying that I am going to take your physical life. What I Am saying is that I Am going to deal with you and lead you to repentance because I love you. This is so important for it is time that you get off of the milk of the word and begin to eat the meat. Trusting in Me for a new car, or a new anything is feeding off of the milk. The visit will come from within the way I came to her from within. My Glory is going to sweep your minds, your hearts, and your bodies and overwhelm you to the point that the flesh will not be able to endure it unless you have the baptism of the Holy Spirit and even then you will need the Anointing of Jesus Christ with it. Everyone receives the Holy Spirit at conversion. My Spirit leads and directs you and reveals all the truth about Jesus that you need.

In spite of the fact that you turn Me off, you reject Me and go on your own way and all the while you claim to be going My way. And I continually work and labor with you. Matthew 3:8-12 'Bring forth, therefore, fruits meet for repentance: And think not to say within yourselves, we have Abraham to our father: for I say unto you, that God is able of these stones to raise up children unto Abraham. And now also the ax is laid unto the root of the trees: therefore every tree which bringeth not forth good fruit is hewn down and cast into the fire. I indeed baptize you with water unto repentance: but he that cometh after Me is mightier than I, whose shoes I am not worthy to bear: He shall baptize you with the Holy Ghost, and with fire: Whose fan is in His hand, and He will thoroughly purge His floor, and gather His wheat into the garner, but He will burn up the chaff with unquenchable fire.' You have no idea what these words mean. Nothing will stop Me from having My way with My children so you need to get ready for the visit. Because if you are not ready you may endure something that you are not prepared for. All this believing that you will never suffer anything is wrong. If you have played with the things of My Word and pretended to be a preacher when I didn't call you and you are now in sin; repent.

At times I have put within you a love for My son, which is the Word, My Spirit, the church, and all others. And this has been only at times according to how much that you have permitted Me to dwell within you. This is why sometimes you don't feel as though you love anyone, or are able to think of anyone outside yourself. You have not lined up to Me or to My instruction book. The touches of My Spirit that you receive even in worship are to get you going in the right direction. They are to lead you into all truth. Not to use as though you have already attained anything. Every time I ever visited anyone in the Spirit even with the smallest touch with My Presence was to cause them to want so much more than they would seek Me more in the Word. And many times these touches were taken so for granted as though you deserved to be blessed if you did any little thing that I had required of you. It was and is all your reasonable service. Yet you took it for granted, took it as though I owed it to you, and took it so lightly that you simply continued on your way without Me. I Am not speaking to all of you, for there are many who truly love Me enough to worship Me with their lives by living and breathing My Word and when they get touched it is confirmation of My pleasure in them.

At those moments that you are doing My will, according to My Word in agreement and accordance with My Spirit, you can feel My Presence. And many, many times you will find yourself wondering why I don't seem to be with you at all times. I am only with you to the degree that you allow Me. I am only present according to the amount that you allow Me to be. You tie My hands and I can't witness to even you that you are in My will when in moments, hear me, moments you turn your own way more times than not. And what do you do during these times? You continue as though you have not left Me. Why? Ask yourself why. Why do you not then get on your knees and repent and seek to be with Me always in everything? I will reveal to you why right now. You don't want to. You live in the flesh and you refuse to come when I call and you expect Me to do it all for you. You have the Holy Spirit and because you do, you dishonor that fact by expecting Me to do it all for you. All the while in this disobedience to My Spirit you claim and believe that you are somehow going to be all right. Please work it out with Me. Talk to Me about it so that I can direct you in how to permit Me to dwell within you forever. It is a growth of faith, a growth that begins with the realization that no, it will not be all right until you get it right. Then you can have the relationship you so desire with Me. Until that day that you let Me in, what can I do? Can you not see that I will never go against the truth of My word and even though some of you may dishonor My Son, I will not?

This vessel fulfilled My every desire but one for years. And inside of her, she knew it. So she brought it to me because it caused her much trouble and she knew that she could blame any person she wanted to but in the end, it had to do with her. So when she came to me she said: "I didn't do it because I couldn't". Then she could feel that I knew better. So she said "I didn't do it because (whatever the self-deception was) of this or that. And she could feel that I still knew exactly why she didn't do it. So finally she saw it the way I saw it and said. "I didn't do it because I didn't want to. I did not want to suffer or endure that even though I was still suffering and enduring." She told me then how sorry she was and asked Me to lead her to true repentance and to never be deceived like that again. And so I did and we are fine now. This is the kind of thing you need.

I gave her a scripture one day and she said she knows what it says and refused to read it. So I gave it to her the second day and she said the same thing. For seven days she told Me that she knew what it said and what it meant and that she didn't need to read it. And on the seventh day, I revealed to her "Do you know Who you are telling that you know what it says?" I did it by not speaking just revealing it to her. And suddenly she realized what she was doing to Me. And immediately she repented. And went to the Word and read it and prayed and go nothing because I did not answer her. Every day for five days she went to it wanting to know what I was saying to her in My word. And then I revealed it to her and she was shocked. There was one word that changed the whole thing in her mind that caused her to seek me farther. And she sought me another seven days and got nothing. Then finally on the seventh day, I revealed to her exactly what I was saying to her and she then understood she had to dig deeper to get the full meaning of it so she went another seven days. Wound up three weeks when if she had sought Me the first time it would have been done in prayer. So you see you may think you know what you are talking about and because you did read the Word you could presume you know it all but You need to make sure before Me of what you are doing.

I wrote this book with a simple message, 'Let Me in!' I will not force you, but I will give you all the chances in the world to receive the truth if you claim Me. That claim gives Me the right to help you. Don't be deceived when you ask Me to come in and be your Lord, I do just that, I come in. Are you so foolish that you don't know what those words mean? A Lord rules and controls your life from the moment you ask. He isn't a leader; He is a King that rules. He doesn't ask if you want to obey, He commands that you do. What happens if someone disobeys a king here on earth? Do they get to give their side of it? His Kingdom is not a democracy where you have a say. He rules and reigns.

If you displease Me, I have a right to do whatsoever I choose with you. I have the right to correct you, to even stop you if I see that you are determined to do evil in My kingdom. What I say goes. You asked My Son King Jesus to come into your heart and He will not rule in unrighteousness. But He will rule according to His Word, according to His righteousness and if you deliberately go against that, you then are asking for trouble. Make yourself safe and be sure. Because you refuse to see it the way it is; because you didn't take the time or the effort to understand your commitment. Because you didn't take the time or the effort to understand what all of that meant doesn't stop the reality of the fact that He is King; He is Lord, and He will rule and reign in your heart because you asked Him to. He doesn't leave you, but you do leave Him. And even when you leave Him He is still committed. He still operates according to that commitment therefore when you need to be spanked you get spanked.

Some say that My Spirit is a perfect gentleman and I will never force you to do anything. It is true that I will never force any man to love Me, to serve Me, or to love their neighbor, or do what is right. But once I come by your invitation all things change. I then have been given power over you. I created you for Me. I Am not created for you. I longed to have someone who would love Me that has a free choice to do so. I have no interest in someone who doesn't want Me. Ask yourself a question. If you loved someone who disrespected you, who never wanted anything to do with you or worse yet neglected and ignored you. Would you put up with it, or would you do something about it?

You can't captivate Me with the way that you are, or the way you captivate others. You can't cause Me to believe anything, feel anything, and decide anything without Jesus Christ. He gave so much for you that I demand everyone who hears of Him to make a choice. I demand respect and honor towards Him. This means that you must have respect and honor for the Word because in John 1:1 I tell you all plainly that Jesus is the Word. And if you never read the word or study the word or ponder and meditate on the word then how can you have Him come within you? You are rejecting Him as you claim Him. Don't you think that is a little insane? You put Him on a shelf, and you go to a church that takes a tiny piece of the gospel and reads it as though it is holy and unobtainable and you live your life under your strength; seemingly, which will fail you, under your guidance which will misdirect you. Or you let some other man who claims to be holy or greater than you or even another woman to advise you. And never does it occur to you that My Word is alive and it is the Living Word. Once you put it into your hearts and minds and you keep it there by faith then and only then are you serving the Living God and you then let the Living Word work within you. And I will then rule. But if you put it in there for all the wrong reasons and allow bitterness, revenge, evil etc., reign in your heart I was invited but you shut the door which you will answer to Me for.

Yes, my love is unconditional. An unconditional love for someone else is never based on how you are treated, how you are talked to. It remains no matter what. This love stands steady, never wavering, never moving from its original position. You love them. They do sometimes painful and terrible things and you still love them. This is how I feel. My love holds steady no matter what is said, what is done. That is unconditional. That unconditional love was given when you accepted Jesus. To continue in the faith is no longer unconditional. You now have to do your part.

Because I love you, it doesn't mean that I won't correct you, nor does it mean that I will not deal with you. And I plainly wrote it in the word that I will not always strive with you. Knowing that you are but a mortal who will one day leave this earth, I strive with you to bring you to a place of complete repentance. Knowing your time is so short. Knowing that the next moment could be your last breath; I strive to guide and direct you into all truth. That is unconditional love.

In Romans chapter one, I describe it plainly. That when you do not like to retain God in your knowledge; when you change the image of whom I Am into something like who you are. When you take My Glory and glorify man, then I give you up to what you want. I let you go because I revealed through all that I made, My righteousness and holiness. Because you never took the time to ponder it, to understand it, to meditate on it and then toss it aside like it is simply some sort of garbage, and you do that continually how do you expect Me to continue to work to get someone in, who doesn't want in even as they say they do want in? The whole time you don't want it you still claim it. I call that crazy! The whole time people who claim me fight against the truth of My Spirit My ways in others and demand for accountability to come to those who are obeying the truth by denying Satan the power to destroy babies or using little ones for their pleasure. All that time they are having gatherings and prayer meetings as they celebrating the right to kill the baby inside of them. Persecuting and hating the truth in My children. Making it impossible for them to choose who they want to vote for by hurting them. I Am watching. I Am not blind. I see the atrocities.

When you are young and unaware of certain things, I seem to sometimes wink at those things you do especially if I know that you are striving to serve Me. But after I have given you warning after warning, year after year, and you still insist on things your way. What would you do if you were Me? I know that you ask what Jesus would do. But I ask you that if you were God what would you do? I know what My Word says I will do. I will require the truth of the Word to live and exist in every man who claims to be Mine. I will require for him to accept his responsibility to take up his cross and follow Me. People do not read the Word because of the conviction in it. They do not want to hear that I will give you houses and lands that you did not buy with persecutions. They do not want to read deny yourself and follow Me. Many will tell you that they do not want to suffer. And I assure you that life is so that you will suffer and endure and it might as well have a reward in Jesus. How foolish that some of you are striving to escape responsibility to the Word. There is no way to escape suffering in this world. With Jesus, He helps you through it.

Paul the apostle knew what he was talking about when he said "Knowing the Terror of the LORD we persuade all men" He knew when the glory appeared and knocked him off of his horse that he was no longer contending with the man. For the vessel who wrote this book, from the moment of our first encounter she knew that she no longer was contending with the man. Of all the things that Paul suffered, he was not afraid of anything. Bitten by a snake; he simply brushed it off knowing it was poisonous and could not harm him. Paul wasn't afraid in prison, he was delivered. He wasn't afraid in all the perilous things that he endured. But he shook and trembled before Me when I visited him within his own soul. His body was filled with terror, which I revealed to him My Glory, and he wondered within himself why he wasn't dead. This is how and why he could endure so many things so faithfully, so powerfully, because he knew the terror of the Lord. He knew no other desire or fear but Mine.

The fear of the Lord is the beginning of wisdom and without it you can face a hopeless place, thinking that it is all right, or it is going to be all right and you can gloss it over or cover yourself with a covering that is not of Me. You can justify your actions and words and make something that doesn't sin a sin simply because you think you have gotten one over on Me.

I am not talking to you about you having a touch of the Holy Spirit. You can be touched and blessed and feel My presence and still not be where I want you to be. You can be anointed to preach or teach and still not be where I want you. And as long as you are not where I want you, you take a chance of not ever getting there. Read the Word, salvation can be lost. You can refuse My call, and reject My Spirit, tramp on My Son's blood and fall. The only way you are safe and your sins are not imputed is when you have all of your sins under the blood Jesus Christ and are with all of your heart laboring with Me.

PART XII

SOME CALL IT AGAPE LOVE

I Corinthians 13:4-8 'Love suffereth long, and is kind; love envieth not; love vaunteth not itself, is not puffed up, doth not behave itself unseemly, seeketh not her own, is not easily provoked, thinketh no evil; rejoiceth not in iniquity, but rejoiceth in the truth; beareth all things, believeth all things, hopeth all things, endureth all things. Love never faileth: but whether there be prophecies, they shall fail; Whether there be tongues, they shall cease; whether there be knowledge, it shall vanish away.'

DO YOU HONESTLY recognize the difference between love and hate? Because it doesn't seem like My church does today. Both are very strong and powerful emotions. The left is driven by fear, which causes hatred. A human being hates to feel fear, therefore, they choose hate to get rid of what they feel. Many don't realize that fear is a witness from their own soul that they are doing something against themselves. You see their spirit feels it and is terrified of what the flesh is actually doing. Fear is a warning to every soul that says "stop!" Don't go any farther. But those who are determined to have their own will, their own way plow on anyway and blame everyone else for their predicament in life.

A healthy godly fear is a reverence that comes before your heart and mind and reminds you of what the LORD wrote in His word that He is not pleased with. That is your spiritual eyes that see and that is what is meant by "having no fear of God before their eyes." Having no fear or reverence for Me or My Son you do what you know is wrong in My sight and your spirit; your very own spirit bears witness to it by causing you to fear without any reason to fear, they have "Fear where no fear was." Is real and it is in My Word. "The spirit is willing but the flesh is weak". When you learn obedience the way Jesus did by the things that you suffer you then understand that there was and is a good reason to fear. "The fear of the LORD is the beginning of wisdom and a good understanding does all they that fear the LORD."

You work and labor to destroy this and sometimes you seem to have made it when you succeed in having your own way. Which My Word says is "willful". the word is "forward". Psalm 18 it tells you that when you are determined to have your own way that is being forward. When you determine yourself against Me to do your own thing in spite of the price My Son paid for you to cleanse you and keep you clean then I decide to have MY own way with you. When you have no pity for what is your nation of children and you have compassion misguided to take care of those I did not call you to take care of. They are not your responsibility.

You may not know it; you may not see it; you may not even understand it but it is written there in black and white for all to see that desire to do My will and want to learn My ways. This strong emotional pull that loves Me is tugging on your heart; while your spirit warns you not to deny Me through fear.

Love as most of you claim to know is the exact opposite of hatred. Hatred demands, love doesn't. Read it in I Corinthians 13. It is an exact description of Me (God the Father) Me, (God the Son), Me (God the Holy Spirit) that is why this scripture tells you that love is the only thing that will live forever. Prophecies will pass away. There won't be any need for them. If you nurtured love the way this vessel writing this book did. If you got into chapter 13 and prayed daily until you could see, understand, feel and know that you had the power by My grace; which is My favor to be able to love through Jesus in you the way Jesus loved you when He died for you. That chapter is an exact description of Jesus Christ and His attitude and love for you that enabled Him to be able to give up His life so that you would have the opportunity to choose to love and not hate.

Many purposes of hatred claim it is because they love. Not so; it is hate that drives them. Fear first that they will not be able to continue in their evil and seem to get away with it. That is why the hypocrites of Jesus' day killed Him. They thought if they got rid of Him then they would not have any reminder that all these things they are doing are wrong. They would no longer be tormented as the demons within torment them because there is no peace in sin. So this feeling that is a witness to their very being from their spirit brings forth a hatred for any reminder that they are going to endure a hell if they continue.

Love goes beyond any boundaries, endures any losses, and suffers any wrong especially in the brethren, but that is not so today. On the earth, no one wants to pay the price to love anyone else. Oh, they use that word, they use it to hurt others to point out they must not have any love or they couldn't turn away the poor when they know these people did not come from oppression, or being poor they came to get what you have without paying a price for it. If it were not so, they would have paid a price to come into the country the right way.

Hatred makes them angry that you have something they don't have therefore they have to take it because they don't want to work for it or wait for it. So just take it. Ask yourself a question. If you call yourself a Christian are you using love as your excuse for hatred when it comes to confessing how wrong you really are in coveting what is not yours?

And you who claim My name cry because others have and you don't. And you think because you are hurting and crying that I Am here for you to manipulate and control for whatever you lust for including coveting your neighbor's jobs, homes etc. Whatever happened to the 'I can do all things through Christ who strengthens me? 'Not the attitude that 'I can't bear it, I can't take it, or flying off the handle every time you encounter something that doesn't please your flesh.' That is what it is you know the flesh. It rules and reigns. Have you ever read James? When you strive and war, there is confusion and every evil work. And like all men or women, it is always everyone else's fault. It is so much easier to never deal with yourself. And this operates in every part of your life.

This vessel that wrote this has been married for going on 45 years. This was written as you see 10 years ago. It is now going on for 55 years. Hard roads taught her to back up and restore the things that she took not away. Lest at any time the ministry be blamed. Whose will do you follow, yours or Mine? Psalm 69:3, 4 'I am weary of my crying: my throat is dried: mine eyes fail while I wait for my God. They that hate me without a cause are more than the hairs of mine head: they that would destroy me, being mine enemies wrongfully, are mighty: then I restored that which I took not away.' I restored that which I took not away. How do you do that? By not fighting to obtain, by not stealing, or coveting, by not hating but by loving enough to say to yourself this person is worth it because Jesus loved them enough to die for them.

I Am not telling you anything about her spouse except that he has learned also how to be good to her and respect her, and he always did a good job of taking care of her. But many times she did not think so. And many times I had to talk to her and remind her of how he took care of her. When you're young it never occurs to you that the person you have chosen to spend your life with may become sick and need you. It never occurs to you that perhaps your looks fade if that is what you built your relationship on then your relationship will fade. It never enters your mind that one day you will be getting older and need someone to be with you and choose to love you enough to take care of you.

Do you cut off the other half of you simply because your flesh is no longer pleased? Perhaps they don't seem to be who you married. Give more love and I can promise you that you will receive more love. Look not on your desires or needs but on the fact that the one you chose doesn't have the ability to grasp hold of the love of Me that you are so blessed with. And that perhaps you are the only one that I can use to love them enough to see My love in you. Many times this vessel fell to her knees with the heartbroken because her spouse did not have the love and comfort that he needed in My Son. Where is your compassion? How far does it take you to understand how My love works? A good man or woman is hard to find and some of you desire a good man or a good woman and yet you do not realize that if you had one in your present condition of mind you would help to destroy them. I Am not telling you to put up with abuse or beatings. I Am telling you to take a good look in the mirror. Sit down and see if your other half has good things about them that outweigh the bad. For what seems bad may be your own selfish desires. Write down all the good things and all the things that hurt and upset you and you may find out that the good out weights the bad.

Take this message as one delivered directly from My Throne. Take it as an encouragement that although you have done so many things against

Me it is never too late to turn away from it. And believe that the power of the blood of Jesus Christ is so powerful that it will deliver you and heal your spirit. For the Spirit within you that is fully, Mine can't commit such sins. A spirit within you that is fully Mine can't bring forth such evil fruit. Let Me change you, heal you and deliver you. For once you turn against Me you become guilty. How did you turn against Me you say?

When I called you to holiness, perfection in heart, by putting the Word in you, you did n't answer, but answered the call of the world the flesh and the devil. I want you, to cleanse you and bring you to the heavenly places that I called you to, not to the ones that you claim you are in. I John1:4 -10 'And these things write we unto you, that your joy may be full. This then is the message which we have heard of Him, and declare unto you, that God is light and in Him is no darkness at all. If we say that we have fellowship with him, and walk in darkness, we lie, and do not the truth: but if we walk in the light, as He is in the light, we have fellowship one with another and the blood of Jesus Christ His Son cleanseth us from all sin. If we say that we have no sin, we deceive ourselves, and the truth is not in us. If we confess our sins, He is faithful and just to forgive us our sins and to cleanse us from all unrighteousness. If we say that we have not sinned, we make Him a liar, and His Word is not in us.'

Take this journey with Me, and let Me lead you to a place that will reveal to you every place that you turned your back on Me. If you are not doing My will, then that disobedience withholds all that I have for you. You search, and search, and search, you believe, and believe and believe and you speak My word and speak My word and speak My word. And some of you have done this for many, many years waiting for a promise that I can't come and answer because you never truly came to Me, to begin with. This is not a one time visit at the altar. This isn't something that your pastor can help you pray your way through. This is something that has to be worked out daily by you and Me to develop a long-lasting relationship with Me. You don't wave a magic wand or say some magic working words and then suddenly change. You work daily and work it out with Me in everything. And while you do that I can and will work on the rest of your life. Up until now, you have used Me and My Word to suit yourself in such a way that you fully expect to have everything when you do a minimum for Me.

I had such great plans for you and up until now you have done nothing but manipulate your knowledge of Me to suit yourself. You sit in a church and some of you are so wrapped up in your ministry or calling, or your supposedly close walk with Me that everyone dies around you. Watching you care only for yourselves; has required much patience on My part. I have been very long-suffering with you. But the day that is here is a day of forgiveness and repentance and making things within your life truly new. When you turn the light off and do your own thing, the darkness is greater than the one who turns openly away and continues in their own way in deep sin.

Your thinking is like the alcoholic that drinks only beer, they have so many reasons to say that they are not alcoholics even though it destroys their relationships with their spouses and children. Even though it corrupts their minds to believe that right is wrong and wrong is right. Even though daily their brains are eaten away and their lives are lived in oblivion. Until there is no way, no hope, and all they have and all they own are destroyed. One day, all too late, they wake up as to what they are and they walk in this life now worse than before if they can't see that they have spent years running away from life. Years running away from the truth, years living a life on a bar stool perhaps avoiding the responsibilities of life and the very basics that they owe to themselves, to their spouses to their homes, to their families, and to their fellow man and their country as a citizen. And they have no clue as to how to make it right. And when they don't seek help in My Word they become worse than before because now they do all those things that they used to do, they walk in all the ways as they used to walk, they think exactly the way they used to think except for one thing; now they are sober and have no excuse. They have now become a dry drunk. They think, act, feel and function according to all the years they spent on a bar stool and life and living passed them by as the brain slowly got eaten up. Now they come to God and use the same mindset. Only now with the Word, they corrupt themselves even more. Why? They receive not the love of the truth. Their pride rules them still for something that makes sense to them and because they never wanted to do it My way they turn to doctrines that destroy them all over again. All because they refuse to go into My Word and repent down to the last deed, to the last word, until it is all finished and worked out with fear and trembling before Me. I Am not speaking of all alcoholics that drank beer.

Go, sit on a barstool for thirty years and go out into life and see what happens. See, if you can catch up to life. See if you are as bright as you thought and good as thought and see if you are able to do what needs to be done. I will tell you; the person who lives with you will suffer and untold price just living with your nightmare if you don't get into My Word and repent. You forced them into a nightmare with drinking or drugs now you force them into another worse nightmare because you are expected to think like a woman or a man and you can't. This is very similar to how the person who lives their life in sin and then goes into Christianity. If you don't truly believe and let Me truly in; you never really change and it is everyone else's fault but yours.

I Am not speaking of any one particular person. I Am speaking to those who know to do good and doeth it not; to them, it is a sin. I Am speaking to those who believe all they have to do is shut things out of their mind. Those who don't understand that no matter what you bury, and no matter how deep you bury it and for how long you seem to succeed, you must give it to Me. Come and talk to Me about it. Not your neighbor who can't help you with this burden. But the One who promised to lift any and all burdens. If you don't release it to Me and cry on your knees, in a godly sorrow for the places you failed. Or for all the times you strove within yourself to do it yourself. That is a tremendous, terrible burden and there is only one release and that is to bring it to the altar of prayer and give it all to Me whether you chose to pray at your altar in your home, or in a church. I will in no wise cast you out. When you come to Me, you are then safe. As you continue in the faith, we work it out together.

But for some of you, oh, yes, poor things come and hold their hand. You who do this, who comfort people in their sin, don't realize how you keep that soul lost and entangled and because unconfessed sin will still follow them to the Judgment, you have made yourselves responsible for another and every person will stand before Me alone. You have family members that have done things they ought not and instead of defending Me and the truth, you defend them in their present condition and they are unable to seek help because they have your support. As a matter of fact, you defend them to the grave. Never considering that the people they hurt needed someone to say that it just wasn't right. But no, you lift those who have done wickedness up so high that you hate people to ever bring the truth out. Is there not even a little a basic understanding of the truth? Can't any of you see that for years before they became addicted, for years they chose to drink above their families? They had to say for years 'I want this, and I don't care what happens to my babies, I don't care what happens to the spouse, I don't care what happens to my job, I don't care that I am robbing them of their lives, their finances, and even their work for they paid me a wage and I was never sober to do the job correctly. I cheated everybody is what their cry needs to be. And if they never cry it, I can't forgive them.

I promised in My word that unconfessed sin will still follow them to the judgment. If they refuse to believe that they are responsible and they continue to deny that they have to humble themselves and admit the things they did and ask for forgiveness. When it is easier to go to a place in their brain that says somehow, some way it will all be all right. Not so. It is according to my Word only. Haven't you read in Matthew that if your brother has aught against you that you first go to them and make it right with them and then offer your gift to Me.? Matthew 5:23 & 24 'Therefore if thou bring thy gift to the altar, and there rememberest that thy brother hath ought against thee; Leave there thy gift before the altar, and go thy way; first be reconciled to thy brother, and then come and offer thy gift. Are you so blind that you can't see that your gift is giving your life to Me? Are you so foolish as to believe that I will accept that gift from someone who has hurt so many others for years and then you say one prayer and never face the consequences or the responsibility to others; that somehow I will just wipe it all clean without you doing your part of the covenant? Your part is confessing that you did wrong; admitting the sin and then turning away from it and never doing it again.

Can't you see that I made it so that you must humble your heart and ask for forgiveness from someone else otherwise you will remain in a continual state of denial until you fool yourself so much for so long that you shut the only door to Me. The only 'way' I made for man was to humble himself before a Living God and ask for forgiveness and humble himself before those that he owes a debt to. Do you realize that I can't cancel your debts until you cancel the debt that you owe to others? If someone has aught against you and they never come to you and they go to others behind your back and gather up through gossip support to destroy you this is not obedience to the word. This is using the word according to your own purposes. To say you were afraid that they were so strong doesn't cut it. The desire to have it your way and gossip to form everything according to your way of thinking is so strong within you that you don't dare go to the person that you imagined hurt you. So you work in darkness with the enemy and anyone else who desires to work in secret with the enemy. The light is where you should have gone directly to that person but not you. You think you have a special thing going with God that I will destroy one of My own on your say so. Oh, you can convince a man or even whole churches but you know and I know it is all a lie to be manifested at the judgment unless you and they repent.

Read it in Matthew, how I forgave a man for all the things he had done simply because he begged me to forgive him. Then he went and refused to forgive someone for the things that were done to him. Oh, I see, some of you are so high, so self-deceived, so proud that you don't need to read the Word. Oh but you do need to read it every day to strengthen the things of God within you, and most of all so that you don't lose them.

In the middle of the night sometimes you wake up and become afraid of dying. Now, why do you suppose you are doing that? You have to push and shove everything out of your mind that tells you that something is wrong. You are pushing and shoving Me. You are striving against My conviction power sent through the presence of My Holy Spirit to enlighten you to the truth that can set you free. I Am striving to reveal to you that you need to forget all of your pride and ask for forgiveness from everyone that you hurt. This isn't a matter of going on doing what you think I said but it is a matter of doing things My way. Jesus Christ the Way, the Truth and the Life. It is My Way, not yours. John 14:6 'Jesus saith unto him, I am the Way, the Truth, and the Life: no man cometh unto the Father, but by Me. But by Me means doing it according to the Word; His Word not yours.

Some of you that have come out of drugs, alcohol or any kind of addiction do not realize that it was a self-centered thinking, a giving into always to self, a way of escaping any and all realities and responsibilities. And you carry this with you into what you think is a new relationship with

Christ. All of your thoughts and feelings center on you as you get into the Word. This is why you apply everything negative to others and only positive to yourself. You are as blind as you were when you turned away from what you were doing in some ways. And the same spirit that led you to drink; now leads you to believe that I Am with you when you misapply My Word to suit yourself and never consider others. I know, that what I Am saying right now seems impossible, but I Am telling you the truth. That until you get rid of any kind of self-centered thinking and feelings, you can't and won't ever learn how to be in My will. Don't let it hinder you. Every person knows within themselves when they have done wrong.

Every soul also knows when they operate in true compassion when they are motivated through compassion. And if you do not check your motivations you can do some of the best acts and they still can center from self. A check on your heart should be often in asking Me to reveal to you if there is anything in you that is not of Me. I will be right there and I promise you that if I reveal to you a problem, I only reveal it to you to take it away through the blood. I do not ever reveal these things to My children to demand them to cry or be so sorry that they ca n't get up. I reveal it so that it can be confessed, repented of and to learn of Me. Some of you can't see that you are in this condition. Please help Me to help you to make it all right. Come to Me about all the things written in this book, just as every man should come to Me about everything written in My word. The Bible is a mirror, as you open it up you can see your own reflection as to exactly who you are. You see where you have obeyed and where you have not. It is to be used to just like that. It was designed to reveal to you what I the LORD rejoice in and find no pleasure in. My finding pleasure in you is one of the most important things in your life. You can please your neighbors, you can please your friends you can please your siblings, your spouses, your boss and anyone else on any ordinary list. But if you don't please Me you never get to where you need to go. And to where you need to belong, which is where you will have joy throughout all eternity.

When you look into the mirror of the word it in detail explains all of that. Some strove so hard to please Me forgetting there is only one way to please Me and that is to believe on the LORD Jesus Christ so thou shalt be saved. When you strive to do things such as work so hard in the church, or with your neighbors, friends you sometimes forget why you do it. You get so tangled in how hard you worked; what sacrifices you went through or gave that you forget what it is all about. And some of you are lost for years and don't even know it. But in the beginning, you knew. In the beginning, you understood. Humble yourselves and come unto Me and I will bring you back to the first works to enable you to get it right. All that this book is about is to open your eyes and give you a reality about who you are, where you are and why in Me. I write many things about this vessel who writes but it isn't about her either.

PART XIII

DO YOU TOUCH JESUS?

And Jesus, immediately knowing in Himself that virtue had gone out of Him, turned about in the press, and said, Who touched My clothes? And His disciples said unto Him, Thou seest the multitude thronging Thee, and sayest Thou, who touched Me?" (Mark 5:30).

And His disciples said unto Him, Thou seest the multitude thronging Thee and sayest Thou Who touched Me? (Mark 5:31)

And He looked round about to see her that had done this thing. (Mark 5:32)

TODAY BILLIONS OF people throng Jesus every day. All are seeking something from Him. Some need a healing, some need deliverance and some want and desire prosperity and many more things. Remember virtue went out of Him and He felt it. Listen to what I AM saying He immediately felt what she was seeking for. He was thronged by those who need and wanted all those things but He paid attention to only one. Out of billions and billions are you one of the only ones? Only one person caught his attention and He looked around for her. Meaning He searched for her. How did that happen, why did that happen? Because of her heart that was searching for Him and His virtue, His purity, His righteousness and all good things in Him. My Son did not answer her because she was in need. listen to all of them were in need of something. Many people don't understand just because you cry or your need doesn't mean you will be heard or paid attention to. Those who truly seek Jesus and the Truth in Him will be heard because they seek Him.

It wasn't her faith but her desire to have the LORD. If you don't have the desire to go to Jesus with all of your heart because you love Him and that you will die for Him. Die to your selfish desires and flesh that controls you. It may seem like your fleshy desires are being met and it may seem like I Am hearing you and you forget I cause it to shine on the just and unjust alike. You only seem to have the power to seem blessed by Me but I tell you a truth today that it will pass and you will have to give up your life that you so cherish more than the One Who died to set you free. It is time for the fear of Me to come upon you to realize how deceived you really are. It is time to permit Me to lead you into the truth into repentance.

In the day that you think that you have Me in your pocket to pull out to use anytime you want and need is a terrible place to be because it will hurt all the more when you are brought to nothing for not seeking Me as I Am and for not loving My Son. Do you honestly think that on the day that you meet Me face to face that you will be able to have any excuse and that you will be able to tell your side of why you kept rejecting the truth in My word? You do know that Jesus is the Truth, don't you? And if your leaders haven't taught you how to live in that truth and they taught you how to get blessed they taught you in error. And you loved to have it so just as it tells of the false prophets and priests did with My children they loved it and enjoyed it all because it wasn't in their hearts to seek My Will or My Son's. O foolish people; you have allowed yourself to be bewitched so that you do not obey the truth. You must get into the Word and see yourself as you are; not as you think you are or as you made yourself up to be in church.

Jesus' Kingdom is not a democracy where you have a say. He rules and He reigns. He is King of Righteousness and LORD OF ALL. As God, I have a right to correct you and even stop you if I see that you are determined to do evil in My kingdom. What I say goes. You asked My Son King Jesus to come into your heart and He will not rule in unrighteousness. But He will rule according to His word and according to HIS righteousness. Make yourself safe and sure. Because you didn't take the time or the effort to understand your commitment to Him and because you didn't go into the word to understand and pray to understand what all of the words meant, doesn't stop the reality of the fact that He is King and He is LORD and He will rule and reign because you asked Him to. He doesn't leave you even when you leave Him. Is that once saved always saved? NO! It only means that He will always work to bring you back to the truth. And do you want to know what that means? It means according to the teachings of His Word that it is better to let you suffer anything here than lose your soul there. He loves you too much.

Bible colleges taught in error on many things, therefore, there are creatures who call themselves preacher teach in error also. Some taught that I Am a perfect gentleman and I will never force you to do anything that you don't want to do freely. Unfortunately for you; you didn't read what some call the fine print in the Bible when you decided you didn't need it. You didn't realize you gave me the right to do whatever it took to get you into heaven. Because you see the blood was already paid and you rejected it in ignorance but I will give the chance to repent always until the time appointed to take your life. For as sure as you live there is a time to die. And whatever state you are in is the state that you will die in and it will no longer be a correction but judgment and I promise you that will be so final, with no chance to repent, and no chance to work it out. You take a big chance in letting it all slide here. Determined to have Me your way.

I don't force you to read the Bible. You say you read it once and that is all you need. And you say that I expect you to use your head; your common sense. You say God gave you a brain and He expects you to use it. You have no idea what those things will fail you miserably; because that is not My Word which was spoken in the beginning. From the beginning of the forming of this earth, I spoke things into existence and I now have a written and spoken word that will remain forever. You see once I come into your life by your invitation the whole thing changed. I kept my covenant and commitment to save your soul even though you completely rejected Me and Mine.

I created you. I AM not created for you nor AM I created by you. Try and understand what that means. You didn't call Me. I called you. Jesus said it. When you believed that Jesus is the Son of Me (God the Father) then it came from Me to enlighten you to that fact. Many people don't believe because I didn't touch them the way I did you. I didn't turn the light on for them to see. No man can convert them no matter what you say think or do. And even when they think they are using My word they don't realize if the life of Christ isn't in them because they played with the church and the word then they have no power to be used to truly convert anyone. The sword of truth becomes a wet noodle in the hands of any hypocrite.

I demand you to reverence My Son. I don't ask for it I demand it from you because He paid for it with His life and I will not allow anyone to dishonor it. Oh, it seems like for a season that you get away with it but at the end of all things you don't. For Jesus is LORD. Read John 1:1 again and see how much of LORD He is.

Don't you understand that you can't captivate Me by your looks, by your personality, by your abilities because I gave them all to you? You can't change My mind about My Word. It will indeed live forever for it is love. Remember I said that all other things will pass away and the only thing that will remain is love. Well, revealing the truth, telling the truth, and anything connected to that is love. All that I AM doing here is revealing My great love for My children whosoever will come and there is no price because it has been paid by the blood of the Lamb Jesus Christ. All you have to do is ask Him to save you from yourself.

PART XIV

DO YOU KNOW THE COMFORTER?

But the Comforter, which is the Holy Spirit Whom the Father will send in My Name, He shall teach you all things, and bring all things to your remembrance, whatsoever I have said unto you. (John 14:26)

WHEN THE HOLY Spirit Comforts you people picture is quite different than it really is. Sometimes the Holy Spirit comes into a service and people shout and dance and sing and praise the LORD loudly and as quick as anything go home and live their lives with all the hell they had before they go to church. What did the Holy Spirit's touch do for you today? Did He convince you of the sins that you know that you are committing daily and continually? Did you allow Him to reveal to you the truth? Did you permit Him to go home with you so that you may go into the Word and repent and pray that you never repeat the problems that face your day from disobedience? Did you let the Comforter lead you into all truth? Did you let Him bring all things to your remembrance so that you can get them under the blood of Jesus? Or did you use the whole situation as though He came to bless you and tell you through His Presence that you didn't need anything because He blessed you and comforted you?

Did you think because you could repeat the message of the day that it was part of bringing things to your remembrance? Or did you realize that you have a great need to repent until all of your sins are under the blood of Jesus? That you are to quit pretending that you know the Word because you remember what a preacher here or there says. Think about it what does the Holy Spirit come for? The blessings flow after His first job is done not before, not during. When you hide your sins you don't hide them from Me and when you cover them with a covering that is not of Me and you refuse to allow Him to teach you how to behave yourself.

Oh yes, My friend He most certainly is used for healing but He is also used for healing the soul. There is so much to be said here but I will only say it to the LORD'S children and not all of you are His.

The enemy of your souls have already studied and studied you and what has been taught in all the aspects of Me. And they came up with scheme after scheme given to them by your church leaders who bought and sold the information and gave it to people that I the LORD did not call. And those people used it to work out a plan to imitate your leaders for themselves to become as they thought more powerful. And for a while, it seemed to have worked. And for a season they have even until this day been able to use it against My children in the government including this President. He is unlike very few of my leaders are in the sense he is actually innocent in My sight. Because before he knew anything that you knew for years, went to colleges to study for years and prayed for years you dared expect him to listen to you who did all this damage that I AM using him to clean up.

You women who have your Bible studies and claim that I AM with you in daring to vet him after years of voting for evil after evil and you are now so blind you could not see if he stands against abortion, if he stands with Israel he pleases Me. Not you, but I the LORD. So listen closely while you foolish women and men have your Bible studies and prayer meetings the enemy of your soul has had a field day because none of you use common sense. President Trump used common sense from the beginning and many of you have the gall to hold him and his wife's past against them. That hinders him daily from being able to accomplish My will. That is how the LORD sees it. Your ability to not be with him proves to Me that you are against him and when you are against him and he strives to clean up this country you are against Me. I don't care how you praise Me, how you think you worship Me, what you think your years of service has done to get you what you think is My listening ear. You needed to take hold of the weightier matters. You needed just like the men in leadership needed to realize if a person is for abortion it is murder and any support for that is far worse than what you think he did in locker room talk.

These so-called great men of God who have their prayer meetings not allowing any woman to attend. Some of you so-called kings sit and have your dinners in an air-conditioned room and are served by the women while women in no air conditioning; no windows, have to wait until you are done with your meetings and like slaves, they clean up after you but none is worthy to be with you men. Let it be known today that is not of Me. You know wild grapes grow and I ask among the Three of Us where did these people come from? We did not raise them? They are the product of their foolish teachers who believe because they do certain things that they are of Me. Not so!!!

I AM OUTRAGED by your actions. By your continual thinking and believing in all that you have done against My Word, against My Son, against My Holy Spirit. While you still have your praises in your mouths you are dealing treachery to My people, to My church. Have you not see it yet???? Do you not know???

Years ago this could have all been corrected and none of this heartache and pain would have come upon this nation. You would have and should have been able to defeat any enemy from within. But when you don't know your way with Me. When you pray for an ungodly leader for Me to be with him as he helps murder innocent helpless babies. Where is your thinking??? Don't you know how to discern these matters? Oh, you poor women you have to stand against those who claim he abused women or did this or that. How about We do this. We totally and completely bring back everything that you did in your past before you met My Son? How about it men, how about if I reveal to the whole world what you have done in secret as a supposed believing Christian?? In leadership yet?

My Word is true what you do will come back on you. Unfortunately for you when you try to apply it to this vessel here. She is protected by Me because she NEVER would have said one word, written one word unless I touched her. And you in the world who think this time you can imitate and use this against My children as I the LORD lead them to repentance. Think again. I AM GOD!!! Whether you believe it or not, I have the power to do exactly as I choose and when I see My children taking heed I will protect them. My great hand will be upon every soul that hears what I have to say, what I think, what I feel, what I do, and anything else connected to Me. Man or woman, they will be blessed in their deed of striving towards a Living GOD, a breathing GOD.

And some of you doomsday prophets who prophesy something I called you to pray for it not to happen and you receive it as written in stone. Some of you who think it is time when you could care less how many hang in the balance as I use this President to clean this mess up? You who dare to take the affairs of this world so lightly that you only think about being seen, heard and known in your messages and none about the atrocities going on daily with My Little ones. Are you going to be held responsible for hurting one of My little ones who believe in Me? It is real that I warn you it is better for a millstone to be tied around the neck of anyone who hurts just one of these little ones. Listen up! They are being raped, ravaged, murdered with great slaughter every day and you have the gall to hinder the only one who wanted to stop it. You in the political parties that play with both sides and call yourselves by My Name remember I AM GOD! As you hold hands and worship with those who call themselves by another name and have another god remember I will not share the Glory of My Son with anyone and that includes you.

The vessel writing this book could feel the fire of My Spirit stirred within her. When she spoke on the first book was when My Spirit manifested like this and every person near her knew that I was in her. But they also knew they could not withstand the fire of My Spirit in her and around her. They gasped and gently said I have to leave the room. They went clear across the large room and told one of the ladies assisting the pastor there that they could not bear to be in My Presence any longer and the other woman said. "You don't have to tell me, Honey. I feel it all the way across the room." Only the Pastor was able to remain.

Right now she still after more than a half an hour she still feels the fire on her tongue, her lips, her teeth, and belly deep within. Magnify that with the people in the room that agree with My Spirit and you will do exactly what these two women did. I explained to this vessel that this is the reason for this kind of manifestation of My Spirit.

"I have come to burn out sin within the hearing distance of every soul who hears your voice. And if anyone feels this in the reading of this book I AM Present to touch you with a fire that will help you to not play with Me.

It will be so powerful there will not be any such thing as you fall back into your old ways. For I will have touched you with My spoken word of today for today is the day of salvation. Understand this doesn't mean that you are perfect. It doesn't mean that you can LORD over anyone. As a matter of fact what it will mean that the fear of the LORD upon you will keep you from exalting self. No one, I repeat No one can call this from heaven, can bring Me down. It takes the presence of My Spirit within this vessel and anointing that she has that I did not and will not give to anyone. For real power is never unleashed into the heart of any man for as the WORD said Jesus knew what was in every man so He did not commit Himself to them.

Take heed to the truth here for it is the "TRUTH" that will set you free. Using President Trump doesn't make him perfect. But it enables Me to use Him for My perfect use. My people need to be free in so many ways. And none of you want to be caught in the crossfire of where you are cause anyone else to stumble from your unbelief.

Oh, you foolish part of the church. Gather by the millions to go against her and try to bring her down. But I will prove one thing that no one can pull Me down in a vessel for I AM GOD!!! There is no other and even though you have those who claim to be the embodiment of Me I promise you that you will discover they are not!

Use this as a guide to discern who is who. Use this as a guide to see in the Bible the things that you threw aside that I counted as vitally needed. Use this to understand how to get back on track to where you belong. For when you find where I AM it is where you belong to all of your needs both spiritual and physical will be supplied. No one who has seemed to accomplish the things of God enough to hurt My children will not have that power. Because of the presence of Me in My children will prevent them without even trying.

Oh, My children, it is not a time for milk. It is not a time to desire to have more. It is not a time to do anything but a desire to do My will so much that you will and do find it. It is a time upon the earth, unlike any other time. For as My children find Me the things in the world change listen to what I say. They change for they can't remain the same as when My children allowed the enemy of their souls destroy while they played. While Moses was on top of the mountain getting the Ten Commandments many sinned so much that they willingly chose to not follow Me on that day. It is a day of Moses coming down off of the mountain with the tablets of truth that will be written on every believer's heart. None can imitate it, none can claim this one for there is no error in it, therefore, it will accomplish what I send it to do. It is not a time to fight. It is a time to LET the LORD take over the way He did for David. It is a time to forget past wrongs and hurts because almost all of you have been deceived and almost all of you have done Me and others evil by your ignorance of Who I AM. In ignorance that I AM GOD!

PART XV

Wherefore whosoever shall eat this bread, and drink this cup of the LORD, unworthily, shall be guilty of the body and the blood of the LORD. But let a man examine himself, and so let him eat of that bread and drink of that cup. For he that eateth and drinketh unworthily, eateth and drinketh damnation to himself, not discerning the LORD'S body. For this cause, many are weak and sickly among you and many sleep. For if we would judge ourselves, we should not be judged. But when we are judged, we are chastened of the LORD, that we should not be condemned with the world. (I Corinthians 11:27-32)

LISTEN O MY children. Communion is exactly what it says. It is a communication between God and His people. You come to Me and confess that you believe that Jesus gave His life for yours, that you believe that He rose from the dead to destroy the works of Satan who held people in bondage through fear of death. That when He arose He ascended into heaven so that you through His body and blood could go into heaven as His. You talk to Him and Me and the Holy Spirit while with all your heart you confess your sins and ask not only for forgiveness but to be led to complete repentance. To wash you white as snow. It isn't done by reading a book written by what you think is some great pastor who understands what you don't. The Word of God is open to every repentant soul. Not to those who use it to copy and destroy what is Mine. It is open to whosoever will repent and be led by My Son and be saved.

It is not a one-time thing to be washed as white as snow. It is a daily working out all the things that are wrong in you so that you can obey the Word. He said to consider the weightier matters. Have enough sense to understand do I care what kind of shoes you wear. How long your hair is. Don't you realize that is "fashion" and it changes through the ages? I said it plainly "do not judge according to the eyes but judge righteous judgment."

Everyone thinks they understand communion. The go to a church and corporately partake communion. Some go every Saturday to confession then go on Sunday to communion and then go out and commit the same exact sins. As though that I cleaned them and gave them permission to continue. Not so, nothing can be farther from the Truth which is Jesus Christ. No one has a special dispensation of the gospel to do exactly as they choose with sin. No one can draw the line, and tell the LORD who died for them what sin is acceptable and what sin is not. The Word is written by man and inspired God does give out the truth that will set you free but even then men make mistakes. First, you must recognize what is a sin. Sin is anything that is not pleasing to God. Ask yourself. Which sins are the most important to God? Does He honestly care what you eat or wear? Do you honestly believe that because you wore a hat or didn't wear a hat in measurement to mutilated babies means anything to Me??

When there are those who belong to Him are being mutilated, raped, and murdered in atrocious ways. Think about it. Consider what I AM saying here. In a neighborhood filled with people, there were some little girls locked up for years and tortured by an ugly horrible man. Forced into sexual slavery and at times when he had people over to his house only a curtain separated them from these girls horror chamber and his friends. Do you honestly think that I cared what anyone wore or ate every day of their torture that you attended church and had no clue in your own neighborhood exactly what was happening?

Churches were all around that neighborhood. People taking communion corporately, people actually fellowshipping, praising Me loud and strong while someone in your neighborhood was tortured beyond belief. Did I care that a woman's skirt was at the knee or below the knee? Did I care that you decided a woman is not as good as a man for that is a man, not I who came to that conclusion? She is not second to you; she is part of your body. (You see these are the decisions that you were making in your meetings.) Did I care that you decided that a woman has no right to the Word of God; no right to a relationship other than that through her man. Do you understand that the power you unleashed was felt by an evil man that gave him the power to do evil to these little girls for years? Do you know that if you truly worshipped Me in church the devil would have no power in your neighborhoods? Do you know why he did? Because you don't know how to use power when you think you have it. You don't know where the line of sin is drawn. You don't understand that My love goes beyond you and Yours.

Oh, I see; you gave to the poor that week. You sacrificed to tithe so that you could have better. You tried to witness to someone that week or you listened to a message from the pastor that had nothing to do with repenting from sin. You can repeat every word because he is such an awesome pastor. You did your duty. You prayed at night "Now I lay me down to sleep, I pray the LORD, my soul, to keep." All the while someone was being tortured. Then on a certain day so that you can take communion before the congregation you sat there and asked Me to examine your heart and see if there was anything in it that was not of Me. You knew, you just knew that I would bless you for being so holy as to even ask such a thing. You knew and were so positive that surely I could see you attended church faithfully. You read your daily devotional and felt My presence. You did all the things required therefore your examination was pure, clean and holy. Never mind that your ears were closed to the cry of others. Never mind that you were not in the place in prayer that you could feel something wrong that I could possibly speak to you to save these little girls.

Oh, I see you gave and supported a Missionary who went across the world to Africa or whatever country and it was as good as you going with him or her or both to reach souls for Jesus Christ. You gave every penny to the poor and now you can sit back and say that you examined yourself and did not come out wanting therefore before all they can see you go up and be partaker of My Son's body and blood.

The vessel who wrote this book went to another state and stayed with family. And during that time she could not sleep because of the spirit that she felt was so strong in evil and she knew it came from somewhere in the neighborhood. So she prayed until I revealed to her that a coven of witches was in the area having their meetings. She had no one with her but My Son Jesus Christ within her. That was two. So she began to pray until I witnessed to her that it was gone. Just the way I did years before that when a Satanic cult down the road from her was raping young girls. And the next day after prayer a policeman came to her home and showed her the mask of Satan's hood and what they did there with permission from someone in authority. There were only two than her and My Son.

It takes thousands of dollars for a pastor to come from Africa and a man who cries that he put his babies in his orphanage to sleep with only weak tea. Yet he spent ten thousand dollars to come to America and when he is here he expects everyone to do his bidding, to feed him like a king and still he doesn't like you telling him what to do with the money your church gave him. Where is that God? Why did he come? Could not that money have gone to make sure his babies had more than weak tea? He comes because you lift him up to be some great Apostle because you have no idea what an apostle is. They tell you they studied this or they went here and some pastor or church person confirmed them but ask yourself a question do you honestly see a Peter or Paul here today? Do you honestly think that I choose those who work for themselves and hurt all others who really have Me in their hearts? They stand at the door and say "you can't come in here we own it". In the day I clean up these things and I will you will all know that I AM GOD!

Who, I ask you who is going to answer for the years tucked away in My broken heart that I heard and saw and felt the atrocity of what was being done right in front of many of you? Who, I ask you who AM I going to visit these things. As it all came out in the news and it is all now forgotten do you think I forgot???? Do you honestly think I have no recording of your hypocrisy in your churches? Do you honestly think that no one is going to answer? Did you think that perhaps these girls must have deserved it? They must have done something wrong to be in that position.

I AM speaking of one incident one particular geographical place. Oh, I know you prayed that the man is brought to justice. How about you? Should you be brought to justice for being partaker of "communion" with a heart not right with Me? Some of you judged those girls in your heart and still do. You gossip and talk about it as though if you point the finger nothing like that can come upon you or your children. Think again! Unless you go on a journey and search out your sins with My Son; unless you completely repent of many sins like this you will likewise perish. Do you see the picture yet?? Do you see the invasion at the door? Do you see young evil men banging down the door of this nation and none of you can figure out why? Corporately you took part in communion. Do you even know what communion is?? Do you understand why I created it? Do you have any clue why I would require you to do such a thing as communion?

Communion is not a ritual let alone a corporate one! It is not a time to play church. In 2012 this vessel had her first radio show which said and I will always remember her telling you the truth. If these kinds of pastors who don't know Me will not repent and step down. I will take their congregations; their money; everything that they thought I blessed them with as they robbed to give to other countries while atrocities went on in their own neighborhoods. All their teachings on prosperity trickled down to the local churches and every greedy man or woman wanted more, more, more. Wanted to prove they were worthy of My riches and glory that can only come in Christ Jesus. After all were you not taught that all that Jesus has is yours?? Were you not taught that all you have to do is claim it. All your problems are solved as you grow in grace.

What is grace to you? My favor? How can I favor such a self-seeking church? How can I protect those who want to protect those who are not Mine and their children belong in their own country, not this one? Wake up. Your responsibility is to your own first in this country. AMERICA FIRST is real in Me. The world has taken advantage of the soft-hearted seeming compassionate American people who have been taught to desert their own and I will be pleased if they take care of those who are not Mine. Listen to what I AM telling you. Can those who love another god be Mine? Can those who covet what you have been Mine? Don't use this to turn on them, or fight them or hate them. But the misguided compassion of My people was from being taught that the answer to your problems is helping those in other nations who want to invade this nation and make it globalist to fulfill the will of the antichrist. You can only help others outside by helping first those inside.

Had you been focused on My will you would have heard the cry of someone right next door to you and been able to save them. I had to reach down and save them but many of you I AM not telling you this to do one thing except lead you to repentance and correct what has been wrong for decades in the churches.

PART XVI

> But the hour cometh, and now is when the true worshippers shall worship the Father in Spirit and in truth: for the Father seeketh such to worship Him. God is a Spirit and they that worship Him must worship Him in Spirit and in truth. (John 4:23)

I AM NOT speaking of the ones who necessarily dance before Me, sing before Me, prophesy, or even have gifts of healings. I Am talking about those who live and breathe Me twenty-four seven, who are never overwhelmed because they learned how to give all things to Me, who are never upset because they learned how to walk content in all things. You know those who have love, joy, peace, long-suffering, temperance, and meekness. Those who never change because of circumstances, situations of life, those who shine with My glory. You know the ones you have sat and ate with or worshipped with that you thought for sure that you never had to be like them for they were close with God and you just didn't need to be. You live off of their prayers when you have needs, and yet you never desire to walk and talk with Me the way they do.

Matthew 13:45, 46 says, "Again the kingdom of heaven is like unto a merchant man, seeking pearls: who when he had found one pearl of great price, went and sold all that he had and bought it."

There are times and a lot of them when the vessel and Myself never speak to each other but we spend a lot of time together. It's a constant flow of revelation. I reveal to her exactly how I feel; and she, spirit to Spirit, reveals to Me exactly how she feels. That language of love that We have toward one another is now equalized on both sides. Of course, she can't love Me the way I do her because I AM God. When I say equalized, it is as much as she is capable of and as much as I Am capable of. You see, she allowed Me to love her so much that I now flow through her, and the love is now returned to Me. She walks in heaven here on earth for we now are together forever. No circumstance, no situation ever comes up that this is not shared between us. There is never a time now that she can't or doesn't hear Me. There is never a time that I can't and don't hear her because We are so close.

She sees Me now as I Am, and I see her now as she is. There is no hiding; there is no deception between us. It is love on love, love in love, love to love. When I communicate with you in the Spirit, spirit to Spirit, there is no need for words. As long as she is in the human, she will always use words, but between us there is no real need. I use words because I understand that she is still in the flesh, but we are so close that when her time comes to leave this earth, there will be no moment of separation. You wonder what that means. How and why would anyone who belongs to Jesus have a moment of separation? When you are not where you need to be with Me and you are only pretending to yourself that you have a great relationship with Me. You will experience a moment of separation. Where the things that you have not gotten quite right in understanding will seem to separate us. You will look for Me but you may not find me quickly and that will cause you to examine yourself and see if you are of Me. Or some sin that you forgot all about will come up between us and you will try as you might pull it down without ever really repenting of it and that will separate us. Like I said before when you see your life flashing before your eyes remember it is real. I AM revealing to you the need that you have to repent. The need to confess, to admit and repent. I can make a moment last seemingly an eternity to help you get your sins under the blood of Jesus.

She found a treasure, a pearl of great price in My Son, and I found a treasure in her. There are those of you who value her, and I was not disappointed in you, for I knew that you would. There are those who dismissed her as nothing because to them they seem so great. But one of the things that kept her going was those who were in need so much that they valued her and honored her. I could tell you so much more because I (the LORD) have so many books about her. That when heaven greets her for all to see, it will be written across heaven what she enabled Me to do in her life.

You see, many of you have a part, and you are not doing it. She calls it your homework. You expect Me to do it all for you. I commune with her the way I did with Adam in the garden, the way I did with Jesus when He had so few words to say, but when He spoke, He was powerful in Me.

Sometimes being in the human, she makes mistakes, and I always reveal them to her before any of it can bring any real harm to her or anyone else. I have written, and I Am writing all this that you may clearly see an example of what I had intended to have with everyone who is willing to let Me walk and talk with them. This book practically repeats itself to make sure that the communication with Me is all according to My Word so that you will not enter into deception. I can't tell it enough. I can't say it enough, for there are those who would love to imitate it; and try as they might, they will never be able to. Copying her walk with Me is not what I AM after. You must have your own walk. Me you must learn your own way. Each one of you has a path to take. She can't take yours and you can't take hers. This is why I don't like you the following anyone just because they seem to have a victory. You can copy and seem to succeed but you miss out on your own. Because I AM God and there is no other and you need me not others. Seek me to learn of Me the way she did. But remember her motives are and were pure are yours?

PART XVII

"And I saw a Great White Throne, and Him that sat on it, from Whose face the earth and the heavens fled away; and there was found no place for them. And I saw the dead, small and great, stand before God; and the books were opened; and another book was opened, which is the "Book of Life": and the dead were judged out of those things which were written in the books, according to their works" (Revelation 20:11, 12)

"And whosoever was not found written in the Book of Life was cast into the Lake of Fire" (Revelation 20:15)

JUST AS SURELY as your life seems to pass so quickly, you must remember that time can't be stopped by you. Just as surely as you are headed for the grave the moment you are born; so it is that you are headed for the Judgment. There is only one way to erase all those pages written against you. Only by faith in the Blood of Jesus Christ the Son of God, there is no other way to make sure that they are erased from MY memory, from MY heart.

Consider this, if you had an only child who always pleased you and never sinned and He knew the only way other could get in is if He suffered and died for them. Then He willingly gives His life to be spit upon, tortured and put in the grave because you as a Father promised Him that they could be saved that way and as a Father you would no longer hold their sins against them. And the people that your son sacrificed His life for willingly, willfully and deliberately turned their back on your instructions to get them into the Kingdom. And they took the word that your son died for and twisted and turned it until you could no longer recognize it.

Then they lie and keep the name of your son, and pretend they do love him before all men but in secret, you see clearly that your son is hated. What in the world would you do? As they sinned every place they could find and lied that you enjoyed it and that it was all with your permission to destroy your own son. They take a hand and agree in prayer that they are praying to the same god as they pray to gods who have no power or authority and have laws that are despicable. Yet as church leaders, they take them in; teach them of Me not realizing that these people are searching for one thing, one way; how to destroy Jesus Christ in you. If indeed you have any of Him while you are doing these things.

When these people are done using all of you; whether it is to cross the border or get into the laws of this country through the government. No matter what they are working to achieve they are lying to you and you love it. You think that I AM with you while you desert this country, and it's children. What in the world do you think will happen next? Do you believe that they somehow remember how you helped them? Don't you know that when you are soulless; when you have no sense of right or wrong you can't be trusted with anything because you have no foundation; nothing to stand up, nothing to convict you that you are wrong or could be wrong.

So when the hammer falls. When this nation falls into the hands of the LIVING GOD (listen up now.)It is a fearful thing to fall into the hands of the Living God. When you play with My Son, My Word, My Spirit, right in front of Me before the Throne and think that you honestly fooled Me remember that I AM GOD! Because in the day that it occurs to you that you could be wrong I will be there. Then you will KNOW that I AM GOD.

PART XVIII

A PORTRAIT OF LOVE BETWEEN THE FATHER, THE SON JESUS CHRIST, THE HOLY SPIRIT AND OUR BELOVED

I WANT TO finish this up with this, for it is a portrait of Our love for her. It shows exactly how I (Jesus) felt the moment she had the victory and was no longer in the bondage of the enemy. I waited many years because when I found her, she was mentally and emotionally ill. She would run and try to bash her head into a tree full force, and with My mighty hand only a second before her head would have hit, I threw her backward about seven feet. She would land on her bottom and get up and again run full force, with her head down to bash her head into a tree. And I would do it again, and she would land on her bottom. Because she could not bear what her mind was going through. To live through her life just one twenty-four-hour period was agonizing, and she had nowhere to turn, no one to help her. She was married and he was never home and his family and her's were no help to her at all. Her mother was in a state mental institution and she was afraid of her father. She could communicate how she felt to no one. (listen to what I AM saying she could not tell one person for no one would understand her, but I did) So when you say that no one could tell because she hid it. You made that judgment not Me. She knew no one would understand they had proven they would judge and condemn her as you did.

She would bash her head into the walls and the floor and then throw her whole body into the walls. And she always said that padded cells were made for her. When she could not endure any longer, she would then strive with all she had to kill herself. To describe what it was like to be her would be impossible. To understand My compassion for her, you could never ever understand no matter how hard you tried. And nothing that you could ever imagine could enlighten you to what it must have been like for her to live through one agonizing day. She was seeing things, hearing things, feeling things that drove her right out of her mind at the age of twenty-four. She lived like this until she was thirty- one year old, and I brought the Word to her. And every day of her life she was alone without anyone to be kind and years later when people had the power to be kind they were given orders by their pastors not to be kind or she would misunderstand so everywhere she turned she endured evil against her.

Everyone around her and in her family and life never mentioned Jesus to her. They ALL claimed to be saved. They now say that is was impossible for them to ever see it but I tell you they did not want to see it. Filled with jealousy, hatred, envy, and bitterness crying how they suffered so. They went to church every Sunday; sat high and decided she deserved whatever evil that happened to her. After all, didn't they do what was right and she did not? Not realizing that she did nothing to deserve what was happening to her no matter what they thought or felt. Because if I the LORD did not hold her responsible for her actions who died and made them God enough to judge someone that didn't know what they knew. Those who looked at themselves and thought they were so much; looked down on her and called her names and said vile things about her that they heard from someone else's mouth. I held nothing against someone who didn't know the truth. But these vessels they claimed the highest they claimed they knew, therefore, they will answer for what they knew when they judged and condemned her and with what judgment they met it will return to them from Me. You see I picked her up because she was so innocent. She was a sinner yes. but innocent of their judgment.

Understand what that means. If you know the Bible and you go against it you are no longer innocent. If I said in My word how I hate judging, gossiping and many other things and you still do them. I hate the sin of being heady haughty high minded people who think they are someone that they are not. And as she strove to do what she thought was right in her limited knowledge and failed doesn't mean she was worthy of their judgment or punishment. And believe me, they punished her for years and to this day they are filled with evil against her. Woe unto the man or woman who lifted one finger to judge condemn and hurt her. She holds nothing against them, she loves them all but I explained to her that I AM GOD and everything depends upon how I think and feel about it not her. She didn't cry to me and say they did this, they said that. She didn't cry out in her pain to punish them. She cried for Me to forgive them because they had no idea of where she had come from. They may find out though. They may lose their minds from pressure because they put pressure on those who were not born into the blessings that they had.

Remember I am speaking about people in the church only. Not about the soulless people who love and serve another god which is no other god. This happened in My sight within the church. It happened within My sight as daily the hypocrites called upon Me and some demanded her to die. I must tell you they are all now dead. ALL claimed to be Mine but NONE ever acted like Mine and if you gather up witnesses to testify what you think she said, what you think she did I assure you they won't pass through your mouth for everything is between her and I and she never brought you to Me. She never spoke evil of you to Me. She loved you; really was sorry for anything she ever thought she did immediately after she realized what she did. But you who decided you were so hurt that I would give you the power and permission to torture her both physically, psychologically, mentally and emotionally. Have a lot to answer for. Judge not lest ye be judged. While she was praying for you to have and enjoy forgiveness you felt so high that she was dirt under your feet.

No, she is not and was not perfect but what she did and didn't do was none of your business. And she knew at least enough to leave you alone. I took her every fault and I covered them with My Son's blood as she confessed them to Me. How dare you not do the same. How dare you take My place and willfully deliberately hurt this Little One who was and is MIne?

I worked with her to the tiniest detail because I saw and knew she could not bear to do anyone wrong. She could not bear to do Me wrong. That is something that many of you take so lightly but she was this way from the beginning when I first met her.

No one else but her and Me, and I would speak to her about everything. She had some dreams and some visions and someone told her that the things she saw were in the Bible, and she asked them, "What's a Bible?" She was thirty-one years old and did not know what a Bible was. Imagine all of the people in her life claimed to be saved and Christians and none of them mentioned My Son to her.

When I found her she was like a wild creature that she had saved one time. A wild rabbit that refused to eat because it was terrifying, and she force-fed it. This was what it was like for Me to feed her the things she needed in the beginning. she had the victory and was no longer in the bondage of the enemy. I waited for many years because when I found her.

She had finally almost lost her mind completely. She could not function, she could not comprehend or figure out how to do certain things and look at people who could and marvel at how they did the least things. So I took her and taught her about her mind and led her out of it like a maze. Each and every day she was in My Word, listening to Me direct her mind, and I healed her slowly like no doctor ever could. No one knew or understood what went on in that brain because although she didn't hide her condition, she did n't know she had one, and everyone did not care enough to know.

And there were those, when they saw her suffer, who was so self-righteous they would think, "She asked for it, she deserved it." And nothing could have been further from the truth. Because those individuals who had a sound mind enough to get into the Word and do what they should have done will never be able to say those words to me without Me saying when they suffer those same words. They will ring in your ears. So I had to come to her personally without anyone or any church. When she was healed, she was determined that no one would ever suffer like that as long as she was around, for she would always tell everyone about Jesus, and she does. So when you read this, you will understand exactly how I felt and why:

There came a great day for her that no one else could see or know and I loved bringing that long-awaited day to her and it was the day that a multitude of people was released.

The day the prisoners were released, My eyes scanned across the multitude of prisoners. There were so many, and they were a sea of faces as far as the eye could see; from the north to the south, from the east to the west. But none of them recognized Me. And then our eyes met. Her's and Mine. We recognized each other. I ran to her, and I lifted her up in My arms, and I held her high the way a parent would run to a child who was tortured for so long, the way a husband would run to his wife. I embraced her with a love that she had never known. With My arm around her shoulder, we walked away, and I paused for a moment, and I looked at her, and I saw that although what she had been through was humanly impossible to overcome, the agonizing torture in her mind should have killed her. She had not changed one bit; the beauty of My Son was so bright within her that she glowed with His presence. There was no memory of pain, no memory of wrong, no memory of anything within her. I Jesus Christ held her head between My hands, and I caressed her face as I looked deep into her eyes, and all I could see was Me.

I cannot describe to you how it felt for My Son Jesus to know that all she had gone through had not changed her love for Me. So we walked on, and to her, it was like heaven on earth as We walked hand in hand. I had so many things to tell her, and she had so many things to tell me, and sometimes I would pause and kiss her hand and look deep into those loving eyes. It was a joy that no man could ever experience know because I AM GOD and you just don't know.

I told her plainly "Blessed art thou among women. Mary was blessed because she carried Jesus in her womb. You are blessed because you carry Jesus in your heart." She would walk through and face all evil and say this to Me. "Father Jesus is so precious in my heart that I will not let the temptations of this would cause me to ever give Him up in me." She would walk by young men in the church who had been told the worst evil of her and the young pastors all listened to the lies and she felt it and walked by as though she did not know. And she would smile and be kind and tell me "Jesus within me is so precious none of what anyone says matters, Lord." She would put her hand on her heart and pat it as if to pat the fact that Jesus was in there.

There are those who think they tempted her with money. It never dwelled in her heart. She obeyed me at all costs no matter what I gave instructions to do. So she never let go of My Son. There were those who knew she would have loved to have more children so in their relationships, not of Me they would try to force her to accept a child out of an unholy relationship and she refused. Being called cruel evil things she endured and will continue to endure no matter what mouth speaks against her.

Could you understand what I AM telling you? Can in your imagination picture what it means to Me (Jesus Christ) to know that she had so little to be able to comprehend; so little to be able to understand, so little ability to do anything but she had a great capacity to love Me? I set all those others free, but they didn't recognize Me when I visit them. I was looking for her in the multitude because she touched Me.

I want you to know that a lot of things that happened to her and against her was too many to put in this book. She was in so many accidents where the angel of the LORD held her in safety. She was almost killed by people who deliberately wanted her dead. She suffered so many different illnesses that she should have been dead a long time ago. And I clearly remember the last one that was so severe and she would get up in church and I would laugh and laugh within her as she danced before Me. And she went home and asked me why I laughed so much. And I told her it is because you should be dead and your dancing with Me. At that time she did not know the seriousness of her physical condition was so grave that at the point of death many times she would lay on her bed and praise Me and have the power to get up and go on with an instant healing enough to keep her until the next time. She wound up with a hole in her belly the size of a gunshot wound to the belly then which more books will tell you all about it. But she overcame it in Me always and she always will because I promised her that she will not suffer from illness or accident when her time comes I will simply call her home and she will gladly come running." (the quotation marks at the end are where I started from the beginning. She did not write this book it is a word for word what God the Father, God the Son and God the Holy Spirit wrote through this vessel.)

The day the prisoners were released, My eyes scanned across the multitude of prisoners. There were so many, and they were a sea of faces as far as the eye could see; from the north to the south, from the east to the west. But none of them recognized Me. And then our eyes met. Her's and Mine. We recognized each other. I ran to her, and I lifted her up in My arms, and I held her high the way a parent would run to a child who was tortured for so long, the way a husband would run to his wife. I embraced her with a love that she had never known. With My arm around her shoulder, we walked away, and I paused for a moment, and I looked at her, and I saw that although what she had been through was humanly impossible to overcome, the agonizing torture in her mind should have killed her. She had not changed one bit; the beauty of My Son was so bright within her that she glowed with His presence. There was no memory of pain, no memory of wrong, no memory of anything within her. I Jesus Christ held her head between My hands, and I caressed her face as I looked deep into her eyes, and all I could see was Me.

I cannot describe to you how it felt My Son Jesus to know that all she had gone through had not changed her love for Me. So we walked on, and to her, it was like heaven on earth as We walked hand in hand. I had so many things to tell her, and she had so many things to tell Me, and sometimes I would pause and kiss her hand and look deep into those loving eyes. It was a joy that no man could ever experience know because I AM GOD and you just don't know.

I told her plainly "Blessed art thou among women. Mary was blessed because she carried Jesus in her womb. You are blessed because you carry Jesus in your heart." She would walk through and face all evil and say this to Me. "Father Jesus is so precious in my heart that I will not let the temptations of this would cause me to ever give Him up in me.

There are those who think they tempted her with money. It never dwelled in her heart. She obeyed me at all costs no matter what I gave instructions to do. So she never let go of My Son. There were those who knew she would have loved to have more children so in their relationships, not of Me they would try to force her to accept a child out of the relationship and she refused. Being called cruel evil things she endured and will continue to endure no matter what mouth speaks against her.

Could you understand what I AM telling you? Can in your imagination picture what it means to Me (Jesus Christ) to know that she had so little to be able to comprehend; so little to be able to understand, so little ability to do anything but she had a great capacity to love Me? I set all those others free, but they didn't recognize Me when I visit them. I was looking for her in the multitude because she touched Me.

ABOUT THE AUTHOR

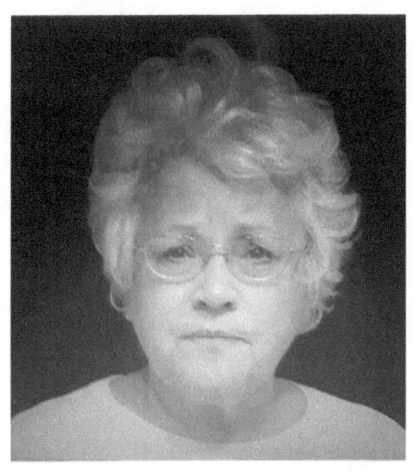

Merienne Lynch began her life in a place of utter poverty in Pittsburgh, PA. One of six children, she lived on a small horse farm. In Aril of 2002, as a mature woman, living in Florida, God supernaturally visited her, which is powerfully chronicled in her first book, "Knowing the Terror of the Lord." Called by God as His prophet in these last days, Merienne began to speak in churches and shared her visitation and revelations on her radio show, "Let's Get Real!" She was ordained in 2009. A prophet's words are to be judged as true or not. Every word she speaks prophetically is established as true to the Word of God! Be prepared to have an unforgettable encounter with our Thunderous God as you read these pages.

THANK YOU MESSAGE

All the praise and glory belongs to Jesus Christ for giving me every word of this book. A special thanks to My Pastor Joseph Anthony Schroeder who is Vice President of the "All Glory to Jesus Christ" Ministries and Pastor Lorraine Schroeder our Secretary. As President of this great ministry I want to thank them for all their support in love and in prayers. Without them I would not have a book or a ministry.

www.ingramcontent.com/pod-product-compliance
Lightning Source LLC
Chambersburg PA
CBHW020123130526
44591CB00032B/392